Commission of the European Communities.

Grants and loans from the European Community

(third edition)

Manuscript completed in November 1984

This publication is also available in the following languages:

DA	ISBN 92-825-5310-8	Låne- og støttemuligheder; Det europæiske Fællesskab
DE	ISBN 92-825-5311-6	Darlehen und Beihilfen der Europäischen Gemeinschaft
GR	ISBN 92-825-5312-4	Ἐνισχύσεις καί δάνεια τῆς Εὐρωπαϊκῆς Κοινότητος
FR	ISBN 92-825-5314-0	Aides et prêts de la Communauté européenne
IT	ISBN 92-825-5315-9	Aiuti e prestiti della Comunità europea
NL	ISBN 92-825-5316-7	Steun en leningen van de Europese Gemeenschap
ES	ISBN 92-825-5620-4	Ayudas y prestamos de la Comunidade Europea
PT	ISBN 92-825-5621-2	Auxílios e empréstimos da Comunidade Europeia

Cataloguing data can be found at the end of this publication

Luxembourg: Office for Official Publications of the European Communities, 1985

ISBN 92-825-5313-2

Catalogue number: CB-43-85-450-EN-C

Printed in the FR of Germany

Contents

Introduction

The purpose of this booklet is to provide information on the aids (grants and loans) administered by the Community to improve socio-economic structures. It is also intended as a practical guide for potential recipients, as it explains how to identify the grants and loans for which they could apply, and how to obtain more detailed information.

Because of this twofold purpose of providing general information and serving as a practical guide, the booklet begins with a general survey of the Community's financial instruments for structural purposes, placing them in the context of the various Community policies. This description, which indicates the links between the Community's financial instruments and its policies, is not a full, detailed analysis, which would be beyond the scope of an information booklet.

Because the information given is in summary form and occasionally simplified, the reader is warned not to jump to conclusions: before the reader is guided through the labyrinth of the Community's financial instruments for structural purposes, a word should be said about certain simplifications.

It is customary and convenient to judge a policy solely from the viewpoint of budgetary or financial considerations. Thus, a country's defence policy is said to be important because military expenditure accounts for x% of the national budget or y% of GDP; or appraisals may be based only on percentage changes over time; or such figures may be used to make comparisons between countries.

This is also true of Community policies. It is often said that the common agricultural policy (CAP) swallows up almost two thirds of the Community budget, while the share given to some other policy in the budget is derisory in comparison.

Things may be simplified even further. A given policy is regarded as being equivalent to the financial instrument which, from this simplified viewpoint, best represents it. For example, in order to compare the CAP with regional policy, the European Agricultural Guidance and Guarantee Fund (EAGGF) is compared with the European Regional Development Fund (ERDF). It is thus hardly surprising that, in the minds of many, regional policy and the ERDF are, if not identical, at least largely the same.

Such simplifications are not only false, they are also dangerous since they lead to judgements that are entirely mistaken. In the first place, it is a mistake to think that all measures under a Community or national policy are necessarily reflected in the budget or in a financial instrument. It would be equally erroneous to suppose that those measures which do not incorporate outright expenditure or loans are less important. It is also incorrect to suppose that a certain financial instrument, by virtue of its name or specific objectives, is the only one serving those objectives. For example, in a given region, expenditure under the EAGGF Guidance Section for improvements to agricultural structures, Social Fund expenditure to upgrade labour skills and increase labour mobility and Community loans to finance infrastructure projects and investments to produce goods and services may contribute just as much to the development of that region as the aids granted under the ERDF, sometimes even more. Conversely, financial aid operations whose specific objective is the development of a region may play a vital part in the development, modernization or restructuring of an economic sector or industry.

These interrelationships between the different categories of Community grants and loans and between the financial instruments under which they are granted are only one of the many aspects of the links between the various Community policies. The connections show that the financial side is not always the most important aspect of the Community's intervention. For example, the Community rules governing State aids and the conduct of firms on the market may, and frequently do, have far more significant effects on structural trends and the development of certain sectors or regions than the Community's grants and loans. In addition, it would be impossible to grant such aids if there were no competition rules imposing discipline on intervention by the Member States.

In those areas where the Community is empowered to regulate the organization of markets, prices, and policy for and even the volume of certain types of production, its measures have decisive consequences for structures, incomes and the level of employment, quite independently of any budgetary implications; and these consequences far outweigh the possible effects of Community grants and loans.

Lastly, in order to understand the importance of Community policies and the impact those policies have through their financial instruments, it must always be remembered that the Community's aids are tied in with the Member States' own financial aid operations, and thus with national policies. Community measures may support, amplify or modify national policies, or have only a marginal impact on them, but the effects of Community policies can never be isolated from those of national policies.

The booklet is divided into three parts. Part 1 provides a general survey of financial instruments in the context of Community policies. Since the aim is to inform poten-

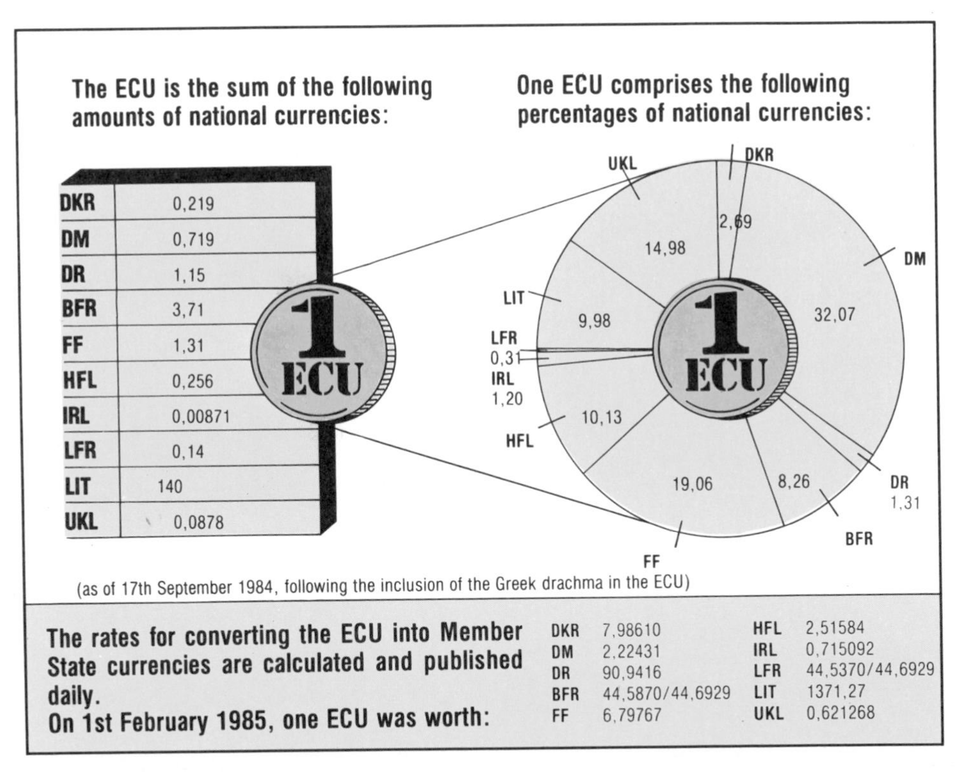

tial recipients of Community grants and loans, only the structural instruments are discussed.

The largest share of budgetary expenditure, relating to agricultural prices and markets, is therefore not dealt with. For reasons of space, the indirect measures under the EAGGF Guidance Section have also been left aside, although they are very important for agricultural social and structural policy. These measures do not establish any direct financial link between the recipients and the Community, since the Community aids are reimbursements to the Member States for measures taken pursuant to Community legislation.

Following the survey of the financial instruments, their objectives and their development in Part 1, Part 2 gives a summary in tabular form of certain aspects of general interest, designed to serve as an introduction for interested persons to the whole range of Community aid schemes. The following aspects are described: the scope of the instruments (operations eligible, sectors covered and geographical scope), procedures for submitting applications and, briefly, payment procedures.

After this introduction, potential recipients will find in Part 3 a detailed description of how the aid facilities which are of most interest to them operate (criteria for eligibility and the selection of applications, rates of aid, etc.)

This booklet does not claim to provide exhaustive information on all the technical aspects of Community legislation; it simply gives the references, and the addresses from which further information can be obtained.

Part 1: General survey of grant and loan instruments in the context of Community policies

It is not possible in this booklet to analyse the Community policies which underlie the Community's many financial aid schemes, especially as all the policies are involved, since they all have repercussions on social and economic structures. Each of the policies which uses financial instruments pursues specific objectives. These are set out in Chapter II, the introduction to the various instruments. In addition to these specific objectives, there are general objectives common to all policies, which explains why the Community now uses an increasingly broad range of intervention measures. These general objectives and their links with the structural grants and loans are described in Chapter I.

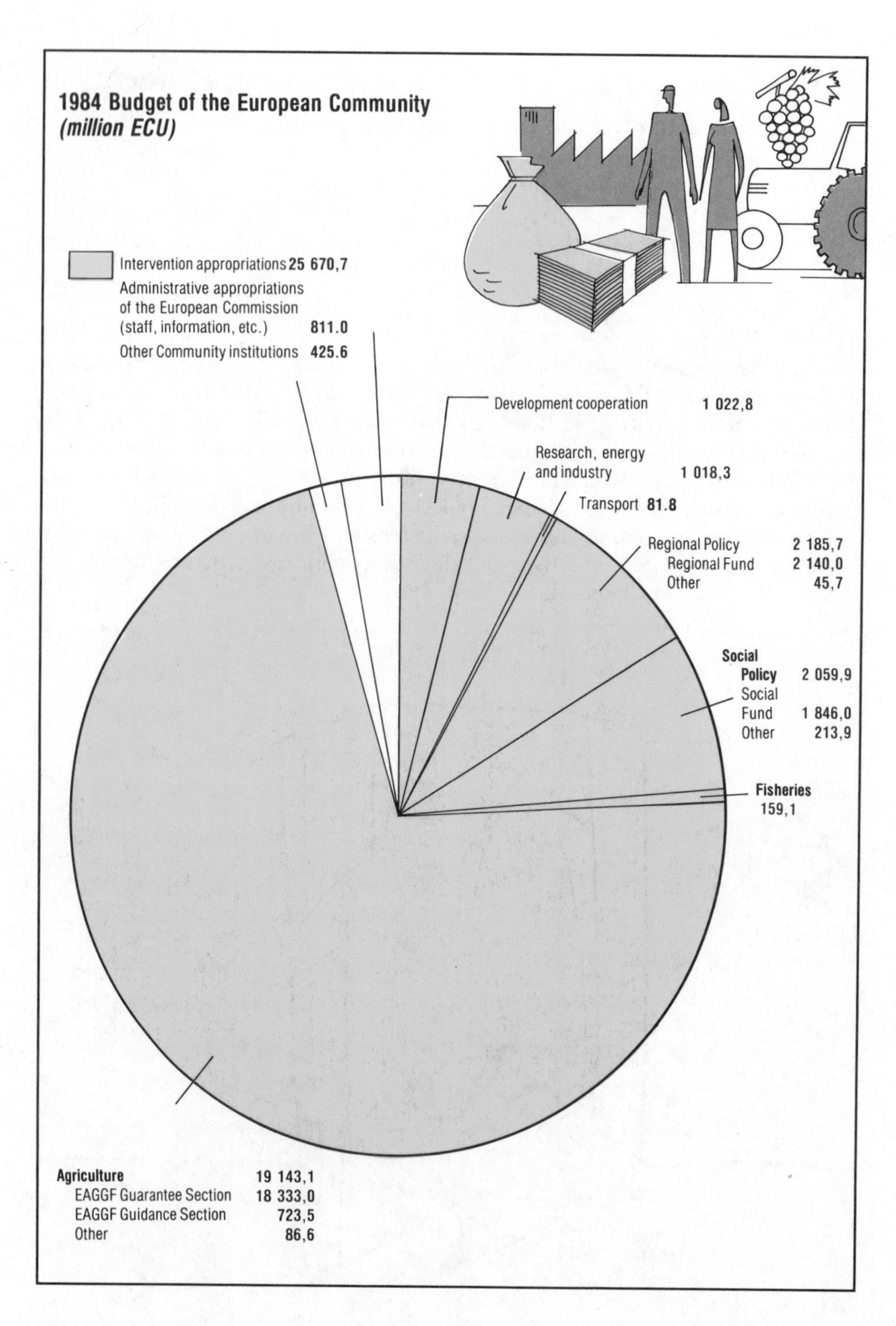
1984 Budget of the European Community
(million ECU)
Intervention appropriations 25 670,7
Administrative appropriations of the European Commission (staff, information, etc.) 811.0
Other Community institutions 425.6
Development cooperation 1 022,8
Research, energy and industry 1 018,3
Transport 81.8
Regional Policy 2 185,7
Regional Fund 2 140,0
Other 45,7
Social Policy 2 059,9
Social Fund 1 846,0
Other 213,9
Fisheries 159,1
Agriculture 19 143,1
EAGGF Guarantee Section 18 333,0
EAGGF Guidance Section 723,5
Other 86,6

Chapter I — General objectives and financial aid operations

The essential objective of the Community is the constant improvement of the living and working conditions of the peoples of Europe, founded on the solidarity and integration of their economies. The two principal means to this end have been the establishment of a single market (the common market) and the development of a common agricultural policy (the CAP).

The purpose of the single market, which is governed by competition rules established by common agreement and has a common external tariff, is to ensure the free movement of goods, services and persons and thereby secure for productive activities and workers the benefits of a vast market on a continental scale, with a dynamic momentum in trade, growth and development.

Similarly, the free movement of farm products under the CAP — based on the three inseparable principles of market unity, Community preference and financial solidarity — is intended to serve at the same time the many objectives of agricultural policy, including better distribution of production in order to achieve balanced development of agricultural structures in all parts and regions of the Community.

Despite the general level of prosperity reached at the beginning of the 1970s, it has become apparent that these means have not enabled all the regions and sectors of the Community to benefit to the same extent from the process of economic integration and the setting-up of this vast market, even though the Member States have made considerable efforts to modify their own regional and sectoral structures.

It has also been realized that national efforts to effect structural changes frequently cancel each other out or pull in opposite directions, because they are planned and carried out in a national context and are therefore on too small a scale. This further accentuates the imbalances within the Community, making certain problems even more difficult to solve and jeopardizing the functioning of the common market.

Apart from the Community dimension to the problem and the need to take action in a Community-wide context in order to obtain more balanced structural development and economies of scale, there is the fact that certain structural imbalances are brought about by Community policies. Faced with such problems — the worsening of existing imbalances or the emergence of new imbalances — the Community must shoulder its own political responsibilities and take steps to remedy them. Its responsibilities are all the greater in that failure to act by the Community could bring to a standstill the policies which gave rise to the difficulties. It would, for example, be difficult to pursue the common commercial policy or the policy of aid to developing countries at the expense of the most vulnerable industries and the least-favoured regions of the Community itself in the absence of countervailing Community measures.

The part played by the Community in international affairs and world trade as a factor for peace und stability, through its action in favour of the less advanced countries and the immense market it affords them, is now of paramount importance not only for those countries but for the Community itself. The Community countries do not have vast reserves of raw materials. Our economy functions as a huge processing workshop. We import raw materials and we export goods and services with added value. Our standard of living, our very survival, depend on that added value. A quarter of the Community's gross domestic product (GDP) derives from its external trade. It is a matter of vital necessity to the Community to secure stable sources of supply and keep its external markets open, while at the same time contributing to the development of needy non-member countries and maintaining the freedom of world trade. The negotiating power of the Community authorities, while greater than that of each individual Member State, nevertheless depends on the Community's internal cohesion and hence on its ability to overcome its own structural problems.

Economic integration is a dynamic process. Not only can it not be halted — or its achievements would be lost — but it must be constantly reinforced and must go beyond the stage of a single market and a few common policies. In 1972, the Heads of State or Government of the Community decided to step up the process of integration: they set their sights on economic and monetary union (EMU). And they had in mind all the progress that still had to be achieved in this direction when they laid the foundations for the Community's regional policy by setting up the European Regional Development Fund (ERDF) a few years later.

For progress towards EMU imposes additional constraints on the Member States in the conduct of their economic and monetary policies and at the same time requires a greater effort to reduce the most serious structural imbalances. When the European Monetary System (EMS) was set up to achieve greater stability in exchange rates, the Community recognized that the burden was particularly heavy for the less prosperous countries and that this called for an even greater effort of Community solidarity. For these reasons, a new financial instrument, the EMS interest-rate subsidies on Community loans, was created (1979-83).

Some of the aid and loan instruments date back to the drafting of the Treaties — the ECSC facilities, the European Investment Bank (EIB) and the European Social Fund (ESF). But it was not until the 1970s, and more especially from 1975 onwards, that these were expanded and diversified, and other important instruments — the ERDF, the New Community borrowing and lending Instrument (NCI) and the EMS interest-rate subsidies — were established. This means that most structural measures are still in the early stages, given the often considerable length of time it takes to bring about any change in social and economic structures. What is more, the beginnings of very many of these measures coincided with the start of the present economic crisis.

The economic crisis — with its effects in balance-of-payments deficits, inflation, slowdown of investment, high interest rates, lower levels of employment, unemployment, our economy's loss of competitiveness in many important sectors and rising energy costs — has confronted the Community with new constraints and new challenges. The fact that these constraints are of external origin, the global scale of the changes in progress and the technological revolution, particularly in information and communications, mean that no Member State can confront the situation and take the necessary action on its own. If we pool and coordinate our efforts, on the other hand, expand the Community's resources and make more efficient use of them and establish new Community policies, we can make this the opportunity of reinforcing the integration and development of the Community.

The Community's responsibility in the face of mounting unemployment and the enlargement of the Community to 12 Member States will occasion further new departures for its financial instruments for structural purposes.

It would, however, be a mistake to assume that new Community policies will necessarily entail, in each case, intervention in the form of Community grants and loans. In many cases, it is enough that the Community, through the processes of coordination, consultation, legislation, overall supervision and information, should create the necessary conditions for firms or public authorities to take the appropriate measures and assume their full responsibilities. Since budgetary resources are limited, financial intervention by the Community for structural purposes can be justified only where at least one of the following criteria is fulfilled: the action proposed is the Community's responsibility and therefore cannot be undertaken by the Member States; it is necessary in order to ensure the proper functioning of the single market; it is necessary for the Community's internal cohesion and in order to secure its power of negotiation with other countries; it is a response to a problem which is so widespread or serious as to have an impact on the whole Community and which can be resolved more effectively at Community level; or the action will make a significant contribution to the process of integration, over and above its specific objectives.

Chapter II — The financial instruments for structural purposes

These are: the Guidance Section of the European Agricultural Guidance and Guarantee Fund (EAGGF Guidance), the European Social Fund (ESF), the European Regional Development Fund (ERDF), the European Coal and Steel Community (ECSC) grants and loans, the European Investment Bank (EIB), the New Community borrowing and lending Instrument (NCI), the Euratom loans and the specific measures for certain sectors (energy, transport, environment, research and innovation).

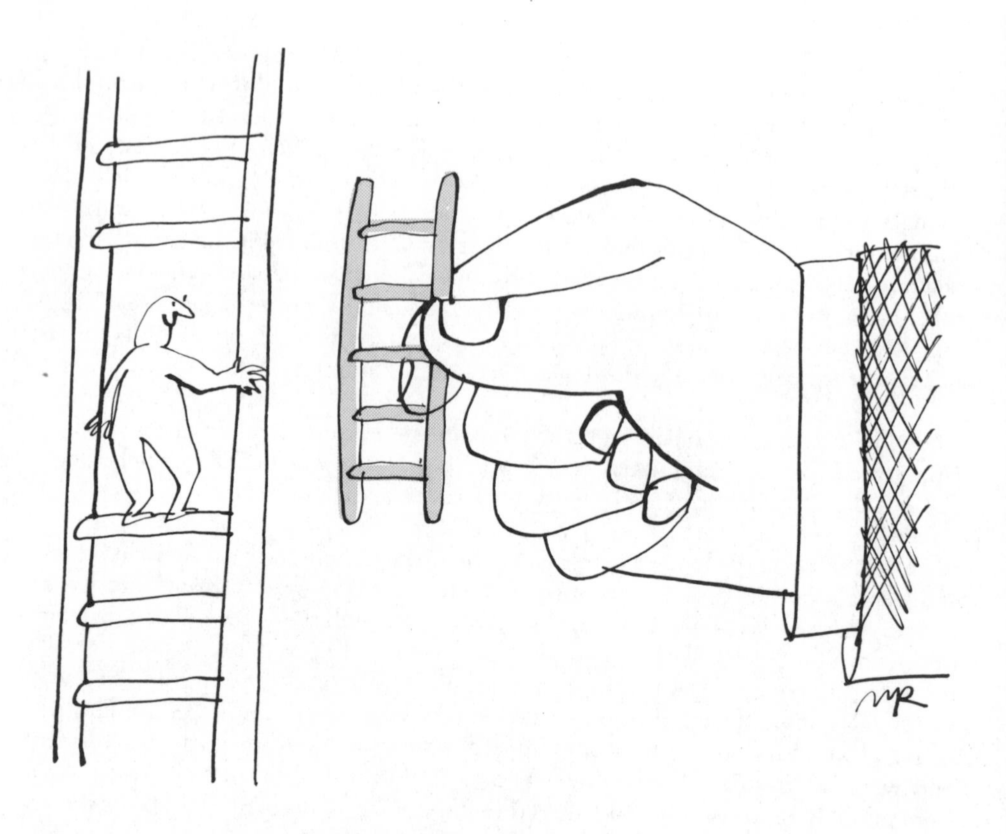

These instruments are complex: most of them cover a range of measures or of aid and loan schemes, each of which has its own particular characteristics und specific purposes. In principle, the three major Funds (EAGGF Guidance, ESF and ERDF) are the main instruments for different structural policies (policy for agricultural structures, social and employment policy, and regional policy), but in fact they may serve a number of policies at once, without departing from their own specific objectives. This is true of most of the other instruments, and it explains why it was possible to demonstrate in the preceding chapter how they dovetail with the broad objectives of all the Community policies.

The following tables show at a glance how each instrument may be used in connection with a numer of policies, and how each policy may call on several instruments. The pluralist nature of the financial instruments shows how Community measures may complement each other and how they may overlap. This makes it easier to understand how, by coordinating their application, the combined impact of the financial instruments can be enhanced. It must not be forgotten, however, that the various instruments came into being at different times, as the policies for which they were specifically designed were developed, and have different procedures and in some cases different institutional aspects. They therefore have certain inflexible and specific characteristics which limit — to a great extent in some cases — the scope for coordinating them in the field.

After the tables, the next section in this chapter is devoted to the origins, salient features and most significant developments of each instrument. This is a general introduction as part of the general survey of the financial instruments and does not go into details. The detailed descriptions are given in Parts 2 and 3.

Financial instruments applied under structural policies

Instrument	Policy
1. European Agricultural Guidance and Guarantee Fund — Guidance Section (EAGGF Guidance) (grants)	Policy on agricultural structures applied to a large extent in conjunction with regional policy
2. Measures to improve fishery structures (grants)	Common fisheries and marine policy
3. European Social Fund (ESF) (grants)	Social and employment policies applied in conjunction with regional policy, industrial restructuring and conversion policy and the policy on agricultural structures
4. European Regional Development Fund (ERDF) (grants)	Regional policy applied in conjunction with all Community policies operating in the development regions
5. ECSC instruments (loans and grants)	Coal policy applied within the framework of energy policy; Steel policy; ECSC social and employment policies; Industrial conversion policy; Creation of alternative employment in conjunction with regional policy
6. Euratom loans (loans) and specific energy measures (grants)	Nuclear energy policy; Energy policy
7. Aid for transport infrastructures (grants)	Policy on economic growth and employment; Policy on major transport infrastructures; Free movement of goods and persons
8. Community environmental measures (grants)	Environmental policy; Industrial policy

9. Measures relating to research and innovation (grants)	Industrial policy; Policy on economic growth and employment
10. European Investment Bank (EIB) (loans and guarantees)	Regional policy; Infrastructure policy; Industrial policy (conversion, modernization and creation of new activities); Energy policy
11. New Community Instrument (NCI) (loans)	Energy policy; Infrastructure policy; Industrial policy (in particular SMEs, dissemination of innovation and new technologies); Regional policy

Structural policies and possible combinations [1] of financial instruments

1. Social and employment policies	ESF for all sectors, ECSC instruments for ECSC workers, and EAGGF Guidance for farmers and farmworkers.
2. Policy for restoring economic growth and employment	NCI, EIB, ERDF, EAGGF Guidance, ESF, interest-rate subsidies, ECSC instruments, transport infrastructures, research and innovation
3. Industrial policy	NCI, EIB, ECSC, Euratom, ERDF, ESF, research and innovation, Community environmental measures
4. Energy policy	EIB, ECSC, NCI, Euratom loans, ERDF, specific energy measures
5. Policy on agricultural structures	EAGGF Guidance, EIB, NCI, ERDF
6. Policy on fishery structures	Specific fishery measures, EAGGF Guidance, EIB, NCI, ERDF
7. Regional policy	ERDF, EIB, NCI, EAGGF Guidance for agricultural structures, and ESF for workers

(1) Possible combinations depend of course on the characteristics of each operation and on project location, since each instrument has its own specific features, scope and operational rules, and the procedures vary widely. Such combinations do not necessarily mean that two or more instruments are used for the same investment project, although combined aid and co-financing are sometimes possible, but rather that they are used to finance separate but complementary ventures and projects in one and the same region, whether or not under different Community policies. Allowing for national aid measures and the resources available to investors, there is no Community region in need of assistance where two or three financial instruments could not be deployed in combination.

8. Policy on major transport infrastructures	EIB, NCI, ERDF, specific measures concerning transport infrastructures
9. Industrial restructuring and conversion policy	ERDF, ESF for social aspects, EIB, NCI
9.1 in the coal industry and in coal-mining areas	ECSC instruments, ERDF
9.2 in the steel industry and in steel-producing areas	idem
10. Environmental policy	Specific measures, EIB, NCI, ERDF

General description of financial instruments

A — EAGGF Guidance Section

The common agricultural policy (CAP) is based on three inseparable principles (Community preference, market organization with common prices, solidarity in bearing the financial cost of the policy) which make possible the free trading of agricultural products.

Financial solidarity amongst the Member States takes the form of the European Agricultural Guidance and Guarantee Fund (EAGGF), which was set up in 1962 and consists of two sections:

(1) the Guarantee Section, which deals with the expenditure required for the operation of markets and the guaranteeing of prices;

(2) the Guidance Section, which came into being in 1964 and deals mainly with socio-structural measures in the agricultural sector.

The Guarantee Section developed apace and eventually accounted for 75% of the Community budget. In recent years, steps have been taken to reduce this percentage with the introduction of a more cautious price policy, the adoption of economy measures and greater emphasis on structural improvements. Guarantee Section expenditure is now growing at a slower rate than budget expenditure as a whole. Expenditure on markets still represents, however, about two thirds ot the entire budget.

Although the Guarantee Section is so important and although agricultural incomes and structures are undeniably affected by the fixing of prices and the resulting expenditure, we shall not discuss this Section here since the expenditure goes directly on markets.

By comparison, the Guidance Section was slow to start and to develop, although it has expanded more rapidly in recent years. From initial appropriations of 50 million u.a. in 1964, the Section's budget has grown to some 850 million ECU in 1984. This represents about 5% of Guarantee Section expenditure.

Although the Guidance Section commands only modest resources, it covers a considerable range of activities and types of aid [1]. Without going into a detailed analysis of all the various types of Community aid, they can be placed in five main categories to illustrate the main features of the policy on agricultural structures.

These categories are as follows [2]: individual projects or direct measures (aid granted to individual investors); socio-structural directives; special programmes for certain less-favoured regions; special sectoral measures (mostly connected with the organization of the market); integrated development programmes. The last four categories may also be described as 'indirect measures' [3] since Community assistance takes the form of the reimbursement of national aid or expenditure.

In all these categories, without exception, Community aid is linked with national aid. From the legal and financial point of view, moreover, such aid is a 'common measure' (Community/Member State) within the meaning of the Community rules. From one category to another, however, the link between the Community and the

---

[1] There are more than 30 types of aid (cf. Table 1 in Part 3).

[2] Certain types fall into several categories, since they combine various kinds of measures.

[3] Certain indirect measures also include direct aid. This fact has not been taken into account, to keep the classification as simple as possible.

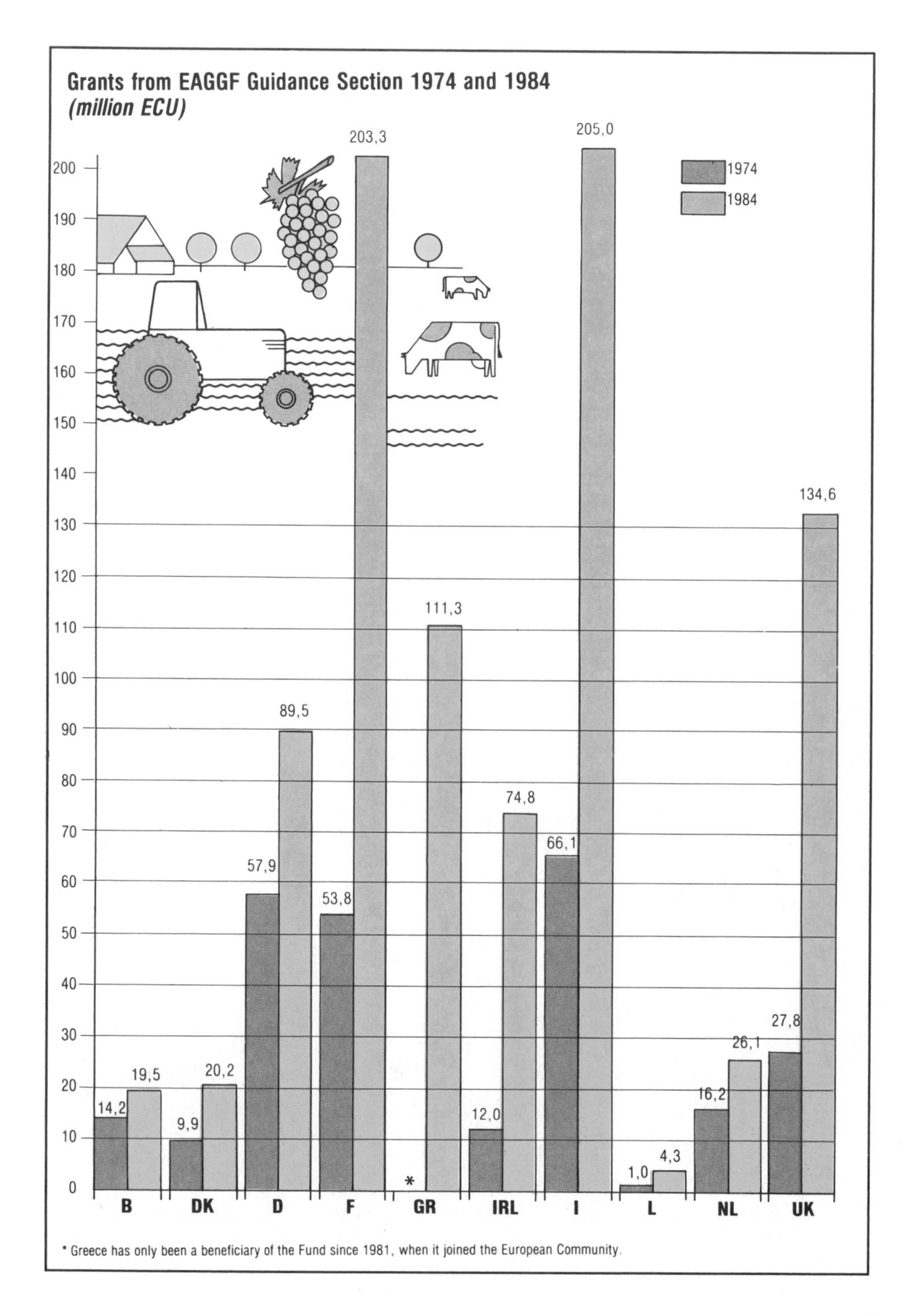
Grants from EAGGF Guidance Section 1974 and 1984
(million ECU)
1974
1984
B
14,2
19,5
DK
9,9
20,2
D
57,9
89,5
F
53,8
203,3
GR
*
111,3
IRL
12,0
74,8
I
66,1
205,0
L
1,0
4,3
NL
16,2
26,1
UK
27,8
134,6
* Greece has only been a beneficiary of the Fund since 1981, when it joined the European Community.

national aid varies greatly, so that the financial instrument may play a very different role in each case.

In the 'individual projects' category, a minimum contribution is required from the Member State, varying according to the type of measure. Under the Community rules, however, the Member States have considerable latitude in the organization of national aid. The Community aid is intended to provide an incentive to individual investors. This is why, in Parts 2 and 3, only this category of Community investment aid is described in detail.

One important development should be mentioned in connection with 'individual projects'. Under the original system (Regulation No 17/64, for many years the sole legislative text governing aid from the EAGGF Guidance Section, is no longer in force), Community aid was granted on a project-by-project basis, but under subsequent schemes, particularly that established by Regulation (EEC) No 355/77 (processing and marketing of agricultural products), the Member States are obliged to draw up national or regional programmes for the sector concerned, as a framework for the individual projects to be jointly financed by the Community and the Member State. Another significant development took place in 1977 when, to take account of particular regional circumstances, higher rates of aid and more favourable terms were introduced for certain agricultural regions.

The main feature of the special sectoral measures is that national aid schemes must (or in some cases, may) be introduced in respect of certain well-defined sectoral activities (e.g. organization of the marketing of agricultural products). The rate of reimbursement from the Community is appreciably higher than usual (as a rule, 50% instead of 25%). Thus, a Community financial instrument is used to constrain, or at least encourage, the Member States to take certain measures, and in return the Community bears a very substantial share of the expenditure. One exception should be mentioned, however. The Community bears the entire cost (60% through the Guarantee Section and 40% through the Guidance Section of the EAGGF) of measures for the conversion of small dairy farms (premiums for the non-marketing of milk or milk products) and for the conversion of dairy herds to beef production.

The 1972 socio-structural measures have hitherto formed the basis of the policy on farm structures. The sectoral measures, and in particular those designed to organize the initial marketing of agricultural products (through producer groups and associations thereof), are concerned with the links between the farm and the market, whereas Regulation (EEC) No 355/77 on the processing and marketing of agricultural products (already mentioned in connection with 'individual projects') is concerned with the links between the market and the processors and wholesalers and, further down the line, the retailers and consumers. Thus, although the aid granted through the EAGGF Guidance Section seems like a jigsaw puzzle of different measures adopted in no particular order and at various dates, there is nevertheless a general theme running through them all which derives from an overall concept of how the agricultural sector should develop.

The structural policy is based on three directives: Directive 72/159/EEC on the modernization of farms; Directive 72/160/EEC on the cessation of farming and the reallocation of the farmland thus released; Directive 72/161/EEC on the provision of socio-economic guidance and occupational training for persons engaged in agriculture.

The most important aspect of these directives is legislative rather than financial. The directives introduce aid schemes which the Member States are obliged to incorporate into their national legislation. At the same time, the directives regulate the other forms of national investment aid for farming, particularly aid for farms which do not fulfil the conditions to qualify for the selective aid schemes introduced by the directives.

The farmers themselves, who are the actual recipients of the aid, are less interested in the Community legislation than in the national laws adopted to implement the directives. As the laws are much more complicated and elaborate, these directives are not dealt with in Parts 2 and 3.

A fourth directive, Directive 75/268/ECC) on hill farming in certain less-favoured areas, was adopted in 1975. This directive introduced a system of aid for agricultural incomes and made more flexible, the conditions under which farmers could qualify for aid to modernize their holdings. The aid to incomes is intended to offset the natural handicaps which beset a large number of agricultural areas. The aim is also to ensure that farming continues in areas where there is little or no alternative employment with a view to protecting the environment and concerning the countryside. The introduction of aid schemes is not obligatory, however, and the Member States have been given wide latitude as to the level of the aid to incomes, although the less prosperous Member States have a higher proportion of their expenditure reimbursed by the Community. The adoption of legislative measures at national and regional levels took longer than expected, and the directives were implemented at a time of economic crisis. It was therefore much more difficult to create, in the regions concerned, a sufficient number of non-agricultural jobs for the labour force which became available as a result of the measures to increase farm productivity.

The directives were made more flexible and were adjusted to make it easier for a larger number of farms to qualify for aid and to allow for particularly difficult circumstances in some countries and regions.

Experience has shown, however, that this policy cannot be implemented in all regions.

The special programmes for certain less-favoured regions represent a first attempt to overcome this problem. One feature common to all these special programmes is that they are largely concerned with creating the basic infrastructure without which the modernization of farms would be difficult or impossible. The Member States are obliged to submit programmes. The Community reimburses a substantial part of the investment cost (50% in most cases). These measures, introduced from 1978 onwards fill a real gap, for when Regulation No 17/64 ceased to apply there were no longer any arrangements whereby the EAGGF Guidance Section could grant assistance towards the provision of the basic infrastructures for agricultural development. The regional nature of these programmes and the involvement of other regional development instruments (ERDF, EIB and NCI) in the financing of certain infrastructure projects provide a perfect illustration of the links between different policies and different financial instruments. This also shows how advantageous it can be to adopt an integrated approach to regional development problems, taking action under several policies at the same time and coordinating more closely (indeed combining) the use of several financial instruments.

The integrated development programmes also stem from the idea that an integrated approach to the development of certain areas and regions is needed. In some places, it is difficult for a variety of reasons, to improve or modernize agriculture or to develop any other economic activity, with the result that no progress whatever can be made. In such cases, an attempt is made to mount an integrated and simultaneous attack on all the area's problems, agricultural and non-agricultural, so as to mobilize and make combined use of all local resources. The EAGGF Guidance Section provides assistance for the agricultural parts of the integrated development programme, but the conditions are easier to satisfy and the rates of reimbursement are higher than they would be otherwise. The Member States may also call on other Community financial instruments for the non-agricultural parts of the programme.

Three integrated development programmes have been launched on an experimental basis, the Council having decided in 1981 to put the Commission proposal to the test. The integrated approach to the development of certain regions could be extended through the integrated Mediterranean programmes.

B — Measures to improve fishery structures

Although the Treaty of Rome had provided in 1957 for a common fisheries policy as part of 'Green Europe' i.e. the common agricultural policy, it was a long time before 'Blue Europe' came into being.

The Community's first decisions go back to 1970. They cover the principle of freedom of access to fishing areas, the common organization of the market in fishery

products and the coordination of the Member States' structural policies, including Community financial aid for modernizing the industry.

As the countries with an Atlantic seaboard steadily extended their exclusive zones to 200 miles from 1975, and with the depletion of fishstocks and the difficulties stemming from the traditional features of the industry, a new departure was necessary. 'Blue Europe' made this new departure in 1973 with the definition of a common fisheries policy. This policy covers four main fields:

1. Access, conservation and management of resources

The basic principle is non-discrimination between Member States and free access to all Community waters (extending 200 miles into the Atlantic). The common fisheries arrangements, which are to last for 20 years, permit the Member States to increase to 12 miles the fishing zones reserved for fishing fleets operating from coastal ports and for vessels of other member countries which traditionally operate in those areas.

The resources of the Atlantic and the North Sea are protected and managed through the annual fixing of TACs (total allowable catches). The Community is continuing to develop technical conservation measures (limitations for certain zones, standards for fishing gear, minimum sizes for certain fish species).

2. The common organization of the markets

The objectives are the rational development of fishing, an acceptable standard of living for producers, stable markets and security of supplies at reasonable prices. The instruments are marketing standards, producer organizations, price arrangements and arrangements for trade with third countries.

3. International relations

The Member States having recognized in 1976 the Community's exclusive competence as regards international relations in the fishing industry, the Community has concluded fishery agreements with a number of outside countries with the aim of maintaining traditional activities of Community vessels or of seeking new resources. The Commission has also been active within international organizations responsible for conserving and managing resources in international waters.

4. Improvement of fishery structures

For several years the Community has been helping to finance investment projects in the fishing industry through the Regional Fund, the EIB and the EAGGF Guidance Section (particularly for processing and marketing plant).

The Commission examines national aid proposals in order to prevent ill-considered increases in capacity and distortion of competition. The Community has introduced measures to improve fishery structures, designed to offer all fishery undertakings an equal opportunity to become competitive enough to face external competition under sound conditions to maintain as many viable jobs as possible. In three years, the Community is likely to spend 250 million ECU on:

(i) adjusting capacity: the Community finances permanent reductions in capacity (through breaking subsidies) and grants aid for the temporary laying-up of the largest vessels (exclusively national aid allowed for other vessels);

(ii) redirecting capacity: the Community may support experimental programmes involving unexploited species or new fishing areas; it may also grant premiums to Community owners of vessels who cooperate with nationals of certain non-Community countries to exploit the resources of those countries;

(iii) restructuring, modernizing and developing fishing and aquaculture: the Community is increasing its support to national programmes for building and modernizing vessels (with priority for replacement investment and coastal areas particularly involved in fishing); it is increasing its aid to aquaculture (with priority for innovative projects) and is supporting the construction of artificial reefs designed to promote the fish repopulation of Mediterranean coastal areas.

C — *European Social Fund (ESF)*

The Social Fund is one of the financial instruments set up by the EEC Treaty, which defines its tasks, the type of aid to be granted and the Fund's contribution (Articles 123 to 125). It was established to improve employment opportunities for workers in the common market and to contribute thereby to raising the standard of living; and its specific task was defined as rendering the employment of workers easier and increasing their geographical and occupational mobility. This was a logical corollary to the creation of a vast single market, which would necessarily involve adjustments following a reallocation of the factors of production.

The Fund started off under a series of constraints. The rules were that the Fund was to reimburse 50% of the expenditure incurred by a Member State or body governed by public law in providing vocational retraining and resettlement allowances for workers who were obliged to change jobs following the conversion of undertakings; only expenditure incurred in respect of unemployed workers was eligible; and reimbursement could not take place until the workers had been in employment for at

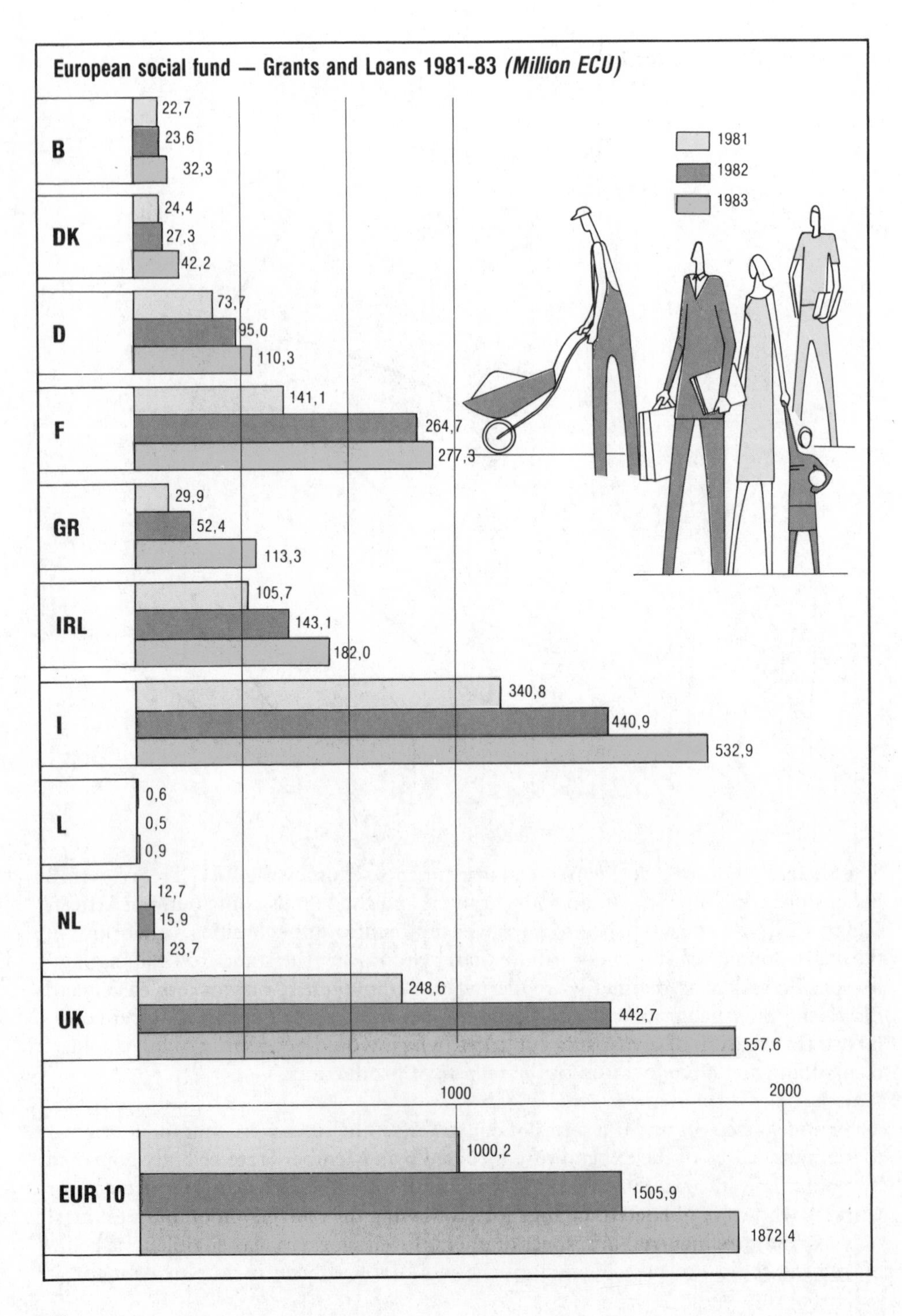
European social fund — Grants and Loans 1981-83 *(Million ECU)*
1981
1982
1983
B
22,7
23,6
32,3
DK
24,4
27,3
42,2
D
73,7
95,0
110,3
F
141,1
264,7
277,3
GR
29,9
52,4
113,3
IRL
105,7
143,1
182,0
I
340,8
440,9
532,9
L
0,6
0,5
0,9
NL
12,7
15,9
23,7
UK
248,6
442,7
557,6
1000
2000
EUR 10
1000,2
1505,9
1872,4

least six months. The Fund had only limited means at its disposal: its endowment was small and its capacity to redistribute resources was modest.

Between 1960 and 1971, approximately 210 million U. a. were granted in aid; after it was reformed in 1971, the new Fund disbursed more than 440 million U. a. in its first two years of operation.

With the reform of 1971, these provisions were substantially amended: the Social Fund was given a new structure and new tasks. It was divided into two sections, one section operating in response to changes in the employment situation in the Community and the other being used to help eliminate long-term structural unemployment and underemployment, particularly in underdeveloped regions and regions affected by a decline in a principal industry.

Depending on the employment situation, the Social Fund acted either to remedy, in certain specific fields, an employment situation adversely affected by Community policies and measures or because common measures were regarded as necessary for certain categories of person.

Following the 1977 review, the operation of the Social Fund was adapted to meet the increase in its tasks arising from a sharp deterioration of employment problems at Community level, and provision was made for aid to be concentrated more in regions and countries with the worst employment problems and the fewest economic resources. The 1977 review also opened the way for two new types of aid enabling the Social Fund to help create jobs for young people; and it led to the introduction of guidelines for administering the Fund, which spell out the Community priorities for each area of intervention.

(i) The concentration of Fund aid means channelling resources to the Community's less favoured regions already in receipt of Regional Fund aid and stopping up the rates of contribution by 10% in priority regions.

(ii) In addition, the 1977 reform also introduced to new types of aid from the Social Fund: subject to certain conditions, assistance for the recruitment of young people under 25 years of age and for the creation of additional jobs which fulfil a public need.

(iii) Commission now draws up guidelines for the administration of the Fund for the following three years. They are revised every year in the light of the economic and social situation in the Community and are used to assign an order of priority to the grant applications.

The Fund's endowment has been considerably increased during the same period. In 1973 approximately 170 million ECU were committed; the 1983 figure was almost 1 900 000 million ECU. However, as the employment situation grows steadily worse, so Community solidarity must be stronger than ever.

New rules governing the Social Fund's operations came into force in 1984. While safeguarding the interests of priority regions, the revised Funds devotes at least 75% of its resources to promoting the employment of young people; special attention is paid to the modernization of small and medium-sized firms; and the proportion of appropriations allocated to specific measures and innovations to combat unemployment has also been increased appreciably to up to 5% of the Fund's total resources.

As to the geographical distribution of Fund aid, 40% of the appropriations available to assist Member States, labour-market policy measures are allocated for projects to promote employment in Greece, the French overseas departments, Ireland, the Mezzogiorno and Northern Ireland. These regions will continue to benefit from a 10% higher rate of contribution. The remaining appropriations go to measures to promote employment in other areas of high and long-term unemployment and/or in the throes of industrial and sectoral restructuring.

The European Social Fund plays a key part in employment policy by helping to finance measures fostering vocational training and geographical mobility and by contributing to the expansion of job opportunities. As already shown in Chapter 1, however, it is not the only instrument to have an impact on that policy.

D — European Regional Development Fund (ERDF)

Set up in 1975, the Regional Fund is of more recent foundation than the two instruments we have just described, but it has already grown apace. The Fund was set up to help reduce regional disparities in the Community by subsidizing investments in infrastructures and production (goods and services). Projects had to be located in the areas and regions eligible for regional aid under the Member States' national schemes; the investments had to be wholly or partly financed by the State; and the amount obtained was to be passed directly to the investor to supplement national aid or, at the Member State's discretion, be applied to other investments. In addition, until the end of 1981 each Member State was entitled to a given quota of the Fund's resources. All these restrictions and the close links between Fund aid and national regional policies might suggest that the Fund's role is simply to support those policies.

Although this would not be entirely wrong, it is not the whole story. One of the most important rules in the ERDF Regulation is that Community aid may be granted only for projects covered by a regional development programme. This has spurred the Member States to draw up programmes according to a common outline prescribed by the Regional Policy Committee.[1] Like the Community's policy on agricultural structures, the Fund thus seeks to do more than merely support national policies: it influences those policies directly by bringing them within a coherent framework. Gradually, as the regional development programmes are refined and particularized through the compulsory annual updating, the foundations will be laid for coordinating regional policies throughout the Community. This coordination process is by no means complete for it took a number of years for the first programmes to be drafted. The concern at present is to make them easier to compare and to incorporate a response to the regional effects of other structural policies, both national and Community.

The rules of the Fund were amended for the first time in 1979 in the light of experience, and the Fund's endowment has been substantially and regularly increased: commitment appropriations amounted to more than 2 100 million ECU in 1984 compared with 250 million ECU in 1975.

These changes included the following:

(i) the rate of aid was increased under certain circumstances for infrastructure investment projects;

(ii) the Commission was empowered to determine regional policy priorities on the basis of the regional development programmes; this was the first step towards the coordination of regional policies in the Community;

(iii) a non-quota section of the Regional Fund was set up in addition to the quota section. The non-quota section was not apportioned in advance and was not

(1) A committee of senior civil servants responsible for regional policies in the Member States and at the Commission. It advises the Commission and the Council as a coordinating body.

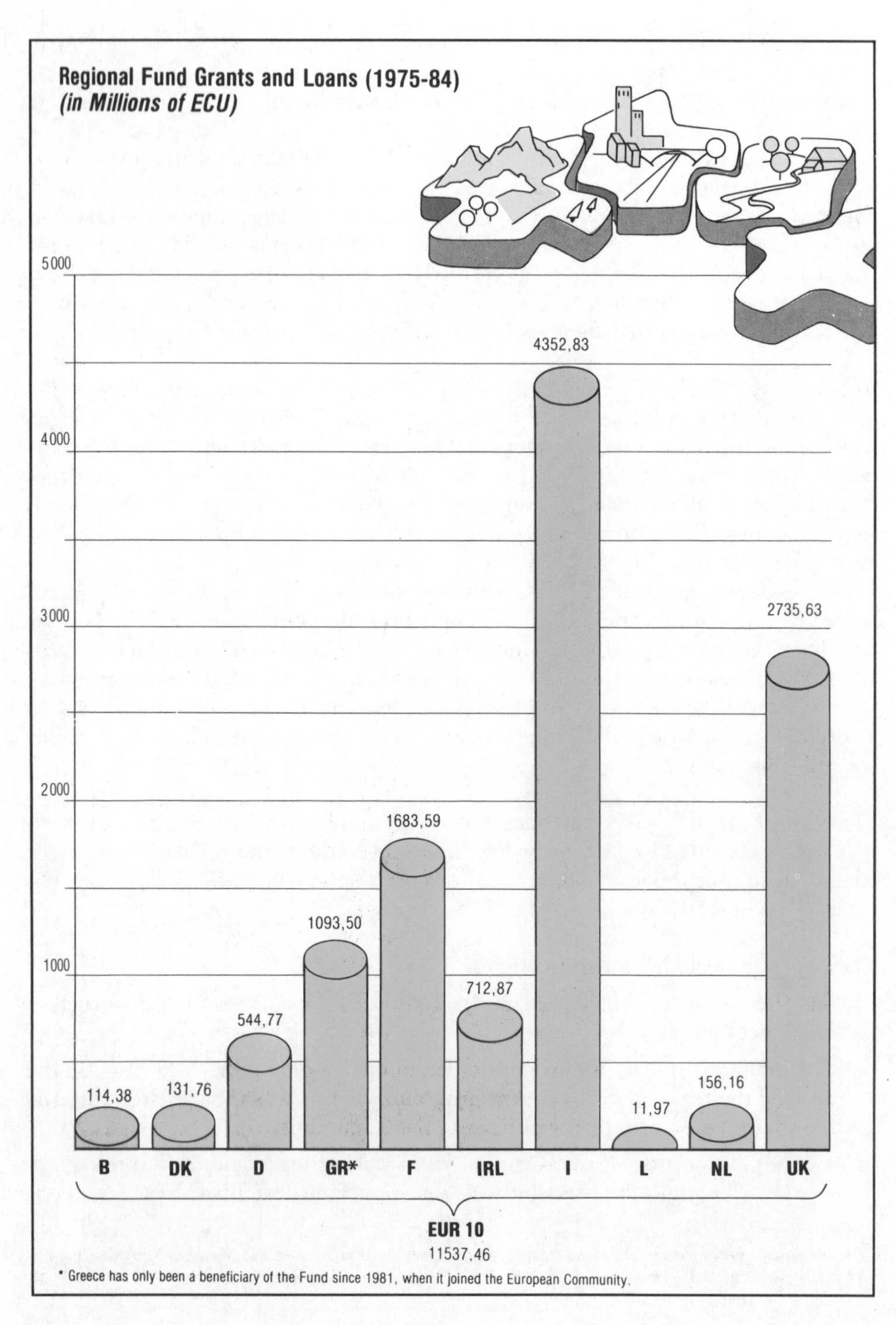

Regional Fund Grants and Loans (1975-84)
(in Millions of ECU)
5000
4000
3000
2000
1000
4352,83
2735,63
1683,59
1093,50
712,87
544,77
114,38
131,76
11,97
156,16
B
DK
D
GR*
F
IRL
I
L
NL
UK
EUR 10
11537,46
* Greece has only been a beneficiary of the Fund since 1981, when it joined the European Community.

contingent upon national policy. It was used to carry out specific Community measures in conjunction with the Community's other policies, either to enhance the latter's impact in certain regions or to forestall their side-effects.

A new Regional Fund Regulation came into force in 1985. It provides for the following innovations:

(i) the coordination of regional policy measures at Community and national levels, which had hitherto only been covered by a Council resolution, is now an integral part of governing legislation. The periodic reports on the situation and development of the regions, the regional development programmes and the regional impact assessment of common policies are of instrumental importance:

(ii) the system of national quotas and the division of the Fund between non-quota and quota measures have been abolished. All Fund resources are now allocated to the Member States on the basis of ranges, whose lower limit is the minimum amount of resources a Member State is guaranteed and whose upper limit may be reached where Community priorities and criteria are fully applied;

(iii) provision has been made for increased participation in programme financing. This is in addition to the financing of individual infrastructure or productive investment projects and of studies. The programmes are divided into two categories:
   (a) 'Community programmes' undertaken at the Commission's initiative and drawn up by the Member State concerned in consultation with the Commission on the basis of a framework adopted by the Council by a qualified majority;
   (b) 'national programmes of Community interest' undertaken on the initiative of a Member State and drawn up by the Member State in agreement with the Commission;

(iv) simplified aid rates (normally 50% but as much as 55% for measures of particular importance);

(v) the extension to all areas of Fund activity of measures to exploit the regions' potential for internally generated development, based on the experience gained from the specific Community measures;

(vi) emphasis on Community integrated development programmes or operations which combine Regional Fund aid with that of other structural Funds. Integrated operations consist of a coherent set of measures and public and private investment projects in a limited geographical area carried out jointly by the national and local authorities in the Member States and the Community, using its financial instruments. The idea is to sharpen and amplify Community intervention by coordinating the deployment of expanded financial resources in the interests of one locality. This concentration of financial resources should make possible some projects that would not otherwise have been carried out and expedite others that would have taken much longer to get started. It is hoped that the economic value of applying funds from several sources in combination will be greater than the sum of the results of applying them separately.

A financial instrument with its changes over the years is therefore engendering a fully-fledged Community regional policy. But the Regional fund is not the only financial instrument serving that policy. As well as the instruments with a very strong regional bias described in this and earlier sections, there are also the Community loans granted by the EIB.

E — *Financial aid provided by the European Coal and Steel Community (ECSC)*

1. General description of objectives and instruments

The ECSC was set up in 1951 by the Treaty of Paris. Although the main purpose at the time was to safeguard peace in post-war Europe, the event in fact marked the founding of a common market in coal and steel, and the new Community was accordingly given substantial powers of market control, in particular as regards rationalization and redeployment in the coal and steel industries. Article 2 of the Treaty of Paris states that the ECSC 'shall progressively bring about conditions which will of themselves ensure the most rational distribution of production at the highest possible level of productivity, while safeguarding continuity of employment and taking care not to provoke fundamental and persistent disturbances in the economies of Member States'.

The financial instruments of the ECSC make up a cohesive system of loans and grants to facilitate and support development, modernization and the harmonious and continuous adaptation of production apparatus in a sector where investment is costly and where decisions by producers in a market economy have considerable social and job consequences for workers. The system of loans and grants is as follows:

(a) loans

(i) industrial loans are granted under Article 54 of the ECSC Treaty towards investment programmes in the coal and steel sectors and in sectors upstream (the supply of raw materials) and downstream (marketing of products). These supplementary financing facilities are usually provided out of funds borrowed, which are then on-lent at the same rate;[1] their role was very important during the period of expansion of the coal and steel industries;

(1) Subject to certain conditions, the Commission also grants aid in the form of interest subsidies on loans under Article 54 of the ECSC Treaty for certain investments (environmental and health protection, research centres, vocational training centres, promotion of Community coal consumption). Overall, these aids have been smaller than those granted under Article 56 of the ECSC Treaty.

(ii) conversion loans are granted for investment projects that will create new jobs for workers made redundant by restructuring of coal or steel undertakings (Article 56(2)(a) of the ECSC Treaty). The new jobs may be either in entirely new activities in ECSC undertakings or in other sectors.
These conversion loans at subsidized interest rates are designed particularly to encourage investors in other sectors to create alternative jobs suitable for redundant miners and steelworkers; granted under Article 56 of the ECSC Treaty.

(iii) loans at a symbolic interest rate of 1% are granted for public-sector housing for coal and steel workers.
These loans are intended to be combined with other sources of financing to reduce interest costs and thus the cost of providing housing, and so to encourage a skilled labour force to settle.

(b) Interest subsidies

These subsidies generally amount to three percentage points per year for the first five years of the loan. They may be as much as five percentage points for five years in the case of the subsidiary conversion loans granted under Article 56 of the ECSC Treaty. The Commission determines on a case-by-case basis the part of the investment (and of the loan) which is eligible for an interest subsidy. For conversion loans, the maximum amount of interest subsidy is 20 000 ECU per job created; these subsidized loans are granted subject to the condition ('social clause') that ex-ECSC industry workers are given priority when the new jobs created in this way are filled.

(c) Redeployment grants for workers (Article 56(2)(b) of the ECSC Treaty)

These grants are made to workers on condition that the Member States contribute at least as much as the Community in the form of tideover and notational retraining allowances for workers seeking alternative employment and wage supplements for workers earning less after a change of job.

These Community aids for workers are an incentive to Member States to introduce similar aids; the aids are combined and are additional to national social security schemes.

(d) Grants for technical, economic, social and medical research in the coal and steel industries (Article 55 of the ECSC Treaty)

This financial aid is granted to cover direct research expenditure, particularly staffing, equipment and operating costs.

(e) Financing of studies (Article 46 of the ECSC Treaty), particularly those exploring alternative employment possibilities for redundant ECSC industry workers

2. Recent developments

All of these loans and grants — which are additional to national schemes — worked very satisfactorily for more than 20 years while the coal and steel industries were expanding and the rate of economic growth made it fairly easy to create new or alternative jobs.

But circumstances are now very different. The need now is:

(i) firstly, in a world of far-reaching economic change, to restore the coal and steel industries to competitiveness and profitability, not only to ensure that the Community always has up-to-date production facilities but also to preserve as many jobs as possible;

(ii) and secondly, to reduce the Community's dependence on imported oil and natural gas and so diversify sources of energy supply, particularly by promoting the use of coal and other solid fuels.

Community policy has swung to meet the new situation, and the changes affect the ECSC financial instruments in four main ways: conversion measures have stepped (hitherto concentrated mainly in steel areas), social aid has been expanded and diversified, restructuring measures have been taken (with the emphasis now also placed on the coal industry) and steps have been taken to promote consumption of Community coal (investment projects designed to achieve rapid and diversified market penetration for Community coal).

Conversion measures have been stepped up as follows:

(a) in the steel industry, conversion investments are now given priority over restructuring investments when budget resources for interest subsidies on ECSC loans are allocated.

(b) The conditions under which conversion investments are financed have been eased: the criteria for granting interest subsidies on loans have been revised and the arrangements to enable small and medium-sized firms to obtain subsidized loans in the form of sub-loans[1] granted through financial agencies have been made more flexible. The ECSC interest subsidies for job-creating investment projects have recently been increased from three to five percentage points for five years under the global loan arrangements.

These subsidies may be granted as far as budgetary resources allow. In areas particularly affected by job losses (ECSC employment areas), the list of which is updated periodically, the reductions in interest rates for conversion loans may be combined with national aid. The reduction in interest rates is also calculated on a flat-rate basis.

(c) Social measures linked to restructuring

The aid provided in Article 56(2)(b) of the ECSC Treaty has been expanded in the past few years. Expenditure on this form of aid is now several times as large

(1) Also referred to as 'subsidiary loans'.

as that on interest subsidies on ECSC industrial investment. And it has been diversified: for example the Commission now helps, under the tideover allowance arrangements, to finance early retirement for older workers and contributes to compensation for workers on short time as a means of spreading restructuring operations over a longer period. These aids have been further reinforced by social security measures taken in support of the restructuring of the coal and steel industries. In order to finance these measures, the ECSC budget has been increa sed by successive allocations from the Community budget.

The move to increased action in the coal industry is epitomized by a Commission proposal for Community financial support for industries producing solid fuels.[1]

Community measures to restructure the coal and steel industries are not restricted to financial assistance. A complex set of Community measures has been implemented covering:

(i) internal aspects: minimum and guidance prices, delivery programmes based on quarterly forecasts;

(ii) external trade policy aspects, particularly for the steel industry: voluntary-restraint agreements for sales by non-member countries in the common market and the observance of price levels;

(iii) general medium-term objectives for balancing supply and demand in the coal and steel industries; and

(iv) controls over State aids designed to facilitate the restructuring of steel firms or the marketing of coking coal and coke under conditions that do not erase the effects of all the other measures.

Restructuring is planned and carried out by the firms, sometimes in conjunction with the authorities. The Commission's role is to see that these plans are consistent with the general objectives and to ensure overall consistency.

Given this approach, loans under Article 54 of the ECSC Treaty can no longer be used simply as financing facilities for firms. First, the loans must not be used for investments that could compromise restructuring — in other words, loans are no longer granted for projects that would increase the Community's total steel production capacity. Secondly, the investments that contribute most to restructuring must be encouraged. That is why the Commission has decided to grant interest subsidies on certain Article 54 loans, selected on the basis of its own published criteria.[2] The interest subsidies, combined with the opinions the Commission delivers on all

(1) Commission communication to the Council, OJ C 264, 3.10.1984, p. 3.

(2) OJ C 73, 18.6.1970, p. 20; OJ C 79, 29.3.1980, p. 2; OJ C 146, 25.11.1974, p. 1; OJ C 343, 31.12.1982, p. 2.

important investments, are therefore now used to guide and even encourage restructuring.

However, this new role has a meaning only in the context of the three inseparable components of Community action-restructuring, social aid and conversion; it must be dovetailed with the entire range of national and Community measures; and the possibility of applying the resources of other Community financial instruments in the same regions must be explored.

F — Specific measures for the energy sector

The 'energy crisis' inevitably made more imperative the need for a Community energy policy. It showed how vulnerable the western European economy was to interruptions or restrictions in supply and to sharp rises in energy prices. It brought out the relative ineffectiveness of isolated or uncoordinated national responses and the dangers posed by lack of solidarity between consumer countries. Finally, it demonstrated the need to shift supply structures away from heavy dependence on imports which means major efforts to save energy, greater use of indigenous resources and the development of energy sources other than oil.

Yet however great the effort to increase the Community's independence as regards energy supplies, imports will still be needed on a large scale for the foreseeable future. The key to the European Community's energy future lies in diversification: diversified needs must be met from technically and geographically diversified sources. This makes it even more essential that trade relations with the supplier countries should be normalized.

The spontaneous interplay of economic forces on the energy market clearly will not alone guarantee that these objectives will be attained. Political action is necessary; while centred on energy, it must cover various fields: organization of the market, research, development and demonstration, international relations.

Community policy has been built up step by step through a series of decisions by Community institutions, taken one after the other in fields where it was thought there could and should be a common and/or Community attitude. This policy is now based on a comprehensive energy strategy.

In 1980 the Community set the following energy targets for 1990:

(i) to maintain the expansion of gross primary energy consumption at a lower rate than that of economic growth and to adopt overall programmes for saving energy;

(ii) to reduce the share of oil in the Community's total energy consumption from 52% in 1980 to 40% in 1990;

(iii) to increase the share of solid fuels and nuclear energy in electricity generation to 70% or 75%;

(iv) to encourage the use of renewable energy sources in the Community's total consumption and, finally, to gear pricing policies to these aims.

The Community's aims can be achieved only through coordinated action on the part of the Member States and by the Community itself wherever it can act more effectively. The measures to be taken cover five main fields, given priority status by the Commission in 1981:

(1) ensuring an adequate level of investment in oil substitutes and in the efficient energy use. Investment in energy-saving and in substitution for oil must be given priority, both as a means of reducing the share of oil energy consumption and because of its favourable effects on the level of economic activity and employment;

(2) developing a common approach to energy pricing and taxation. The aim is to ensure that prices truly correspond to long-term market conditions and costs. Greater transparency of prices and tariffs will therefore be sought. There must also be a common effort to adapt oil taxation to the aims of the Community's energy and economic policies;

(3) adopting measures to give practical expression to Community solidarity in order to avoid instability on the market. The aim is to ensure that a slight squeeze in oil supplies does not trigger off disproportionate fluctuations in oil prices. The

measures proposed are intended to strengthen Community solidarity and supplement the arrangements already set up to deal with serious supply difficulties. The question of security of supply also arises, although in different terms, for other sources of energy: the Community must address itself to this problem;

(4) strengthening the common policies in the fields of research and development and technological demonstration. Innovation is a necessary part of the energy strategy. Financial action and coordination at Community level are vital for obtaining effective results in R&D and technological demonstration in the Community. The Community's potential in this field must be exploited to the full;

(5) developing common approaches and initiatives as regards external relations in the energy field. The Community, which alone provides the necessary dimension for the expression of the Member States' interests on the world stage, must etablish, with the countries which provide its energy supplies, a framework of relations which ensure stable supplies. Where energy cooperation with the developing countries is concerned, the Commission wishes to exploit to the full the possibilities afforded by the Lomé Convention and to step up its efforts to help the developing countries.

Laws and regulations are not the only means to these ends: major financial support is also being given for research and investment.

The European Community is contributing to this financial effort in a number of ways:

- Firstly, it is devoting a large share of the resources available under its financial instruments to the energy sector. The Community is already helping to finance nuclear power stations, the production and transportation of hydrocarbons (oil and gas pipelines), the equipping and modernization of coal mines, the conversion of oil-burning plants to coal, the linking up of Community electricity grids and of those with grids in neighbouring countries, and various energy saving projects, with particular emphasis on industry, public buildings and district heating. In 1983, the loans granted to the energy sector by the ECSC, Euratom, the European Investment Bank and the New Community Instrument for borrowing and lending (NCI) totalled some 2 700 million ECU.
- The Community is also involved in joint research programmes on coal and nuclear energy as well as on new energy sources. In 1983, total Community appropriations for research, industrial development and demonstration in the energy sector exceeded 400 million ECU. Community financing accounts for some 10% of the total public aid given to energy research in Europe, thereby ensuring coordination of a much larger proportion of European research activities.
- Finally, at the stage between scientific research and the application of tried and tested techniques, the Community contributes to specific technological development projects and demonstration projects. These projects cover the technology

for exploiting hydrocarbons, coal gasification and liquefaction, energy conservation, and the exploitation of renewable energy sources such as solar and geothermal energy. In March 1984, the Council of Ministers authorized the Community to allocate 295 million ECU to demonstration projects from 1983 to 1985.

Because they are examined and administered in a Community-wide context, these projects can be selected over a wide range (through invitations to tender published in the *Official Journal of the European Communities)*, duplication be avoided and the pooling of efforts encouraged, adequate financial support can be granted on the basis of common principles for projects aimed at resolving problems arising in all the Member States, and the opportunities for disseminating and marketing new technologies over the entire European market are increased.

G — Special aid for transport infrastructure

A key economic sector, transport accounts for some 6,5% of the Community's gross national product and provides jobs for more than 6 million people. As long as 1957, the Community sought to organize a common market in inland transport in accordance with the aims laid down in the Treaty of Rome. After the first enlargement of the Community action in this sector was redefined. A programme adopted for the period 1973-77 was extended until 1983, in which year the Commission published several communications to the Council of Ministers. Its aim was to galvanize the common transport policy.

For although some 170 Community texts were adopted in the span of a quarter of a century and some decisive steps were taken towards the unification of the European transport market, progress has been very slow and has fallen well short of expectations. Condemned by the European Parliament, which has brought an action before the Court of Justice against the Council for failure to act, the absence of a real common transport policy is all the more regrettable in that:

(i) It is in the interests of member countries to derive maximum benefit from the considerable public and private investment devoted to transport. The differences between national policies affect efficiency, profitability and productivity. Only the Community can ensure that national programmes, are compatible, harmonize them as required and so achieve economies of scale. It can also provide technical or financial assistance for projects concerning two or more Member States.

(ii) The success of most Community policies (agriculture, industry, regional development, energy, environment, tourism, etc.) heavily depends on the quality of transport services on Community territory.

(iii) The elimination of distortions of competition and discrimination against various categories of carrier is an essential precondition for the actual application of

the basic principle of the common market: the free movement of goods and persons.

The Commission has therefore set the following major objectives for the years ahead:

(i) greater integration of national transport policies;

(ii) improved conditions of competition between and within the various modes of transport;

(iii) increased productivity and efficiency of the European transport system, with an attack on bottlenecks and regulatory constraints on the market;

(iv) assistance to the financing of major infrastructure projects of benefit to the Community.

The Community has for a long time been financing certain national transport infrastructure projects. Between 1958 and the end of 1983, loans for this purpose from the European Investment Bank and the New Community Instrument totalled more than 2 700 million ECU and from the European Regional Development Fund totalled approximately 2 300 million ECU between 1975 (when the Fund was set up) and the end of 1983. The common aid is to promote the development of the less-favoured regions and also, in the case of the EIB and the NCI, to improve communications between Community countries.

However, more must be done. The Community has a role to play in planning and financing the new transport infrastructure needed to meet the present and future requirements, seen from a Community perspective. The Community interest must be taken into account when new projects are planned. In particular, steps should be taken to ensure that national projects are mutually compatible, to remove bottlenecks in intra-Community transport and to promote the gradual integration of the European network. Finally, a contribution must be made to projects which provide social and economic benefits for the Community but which would be difficult to carry out without Community aid. The Commission accordingly proposed in 1976 that a specific financial instrument be set up to provide grants or low-interest loans for projects of Community interest. The Council of Ministers has not yet agreed to set up a permanent instrument of this kind, but the idea has already led to:

(i) limited measures under which the Community allocated 10 million ECU in 1982 to the Domodossola marshalling yard and customs clearance station (Italy), a section of the Evzoni-Volos trunk road (Greece) and an evaluation study on the financing of a fixed cross-Channel link;

(ii) a Commission proposal for a multiannual experimental programme of special aid for transport infrastructures.
This proposal has begun to have practical effect in the form of a Council Regulation on projects receiving Community financial support under the 1983 and 1984 budgets.

H — Community measures for the environment

The need for a Community policy on the environment was proclaimed by the Community Heads of State or Government at their summit meeting in Paris in October 1972. A series of action programmes have since been adopted.

The Community's environment policy has three objectives: to protect human health; to safeguard the long-term availability and quality of all the resources which determine the human environment, namely water, air, space, ambient factors in general, raw materials, the human-settlement environment, and landscape and countryside; to maintain and, where possible, restore the natural environment and suitable habitats for plant and animal wildlife.

The interdependence of these various resources requires an overall strategy — a strategy which must increasingly take a preventive form. The fight against pollution and the degradation of scarce resources is less expensive, more effective and more conducive to sound economic development if environmental needs are taken into account from the very beginning of the planning and decision-making process, whether in agriculture, energy, industry, transport or tourism.

The Community must therefore:

(i) promote scientific research so as to improve preparation of the necessary measures;

(ii) establish Community rules for the protection of environmental resources and monitor their application;

(iii) improve information, training and public awareness of environmental problems;

(iv) promote procedures for ensuring that environmental questions are taken into account before any decision liable to affect the environment is taken. Community directives concerning dangerous substances already provide for authorization or control procedures before products are placed on the market. The Commission has presented a proposal whereby an environmental impact assessment must be made before major industrial and infrastructure works can be undertaken. Environmental impact is already taken into account in the financing decisions of the European Investment Bank and the Community's other financial instruments;

(v) have financial resources at its disposal. In order to reduce pollution without introducing distortions of competition, the Community adopted in 1975 the 'polluter pays' principle, that the polluter must bear the cost of preventing or eliminating pollution. As, however, in current economic conditions firms frequently cannot bear additional costs, the Commission has authorized the granting of public aid for reducing pollution for a limited period and subject to certain conditions. The Commission also wishes to step up the financial contribution which the Community already makes for environmental purposes through its agricultural and regional Funds and the European Investment Bank.
A large number of infrastructure projects have been financed, for example a purifying plant and the protection and cleansing of the Gulf of Naples and other coastal areas. Each year the ERDF grants average aid totalling between 150 and

170 million ECU for such projects. The EIB has granted loans for such purposes totalling more than 1 600 million ECU since 1958 (not counting investments connected with projects financed in other fields).

Since 1984, the Community has also been implementing special measures in the environmental field by granting aid to three categories of project:

(i) demonstration projects to develop new clean technologies (i.e. causing little or no pollution and more sparing of natural resources) in specific fields;

(ii) demonstration projects to develop new techniques and methods of measuring and monitoring the quality of the natural environment;

(iii) projects to encourage the preservation or re-establishment of seriously threatened habitats of endangered species of special importance for the Community under Directive 79/409/EEC.

The use of all these legislative instruments and financial resources will contribute to economic development with more harmonious and better-balanced aims and to an improvement in the quality of life.

I — Measures relating to research and innovation [1]

Against the current background of economic change, the European Community is less competitive than its main rivals in the industrialized world, Japan and the United States. The new strategies proposed by the Commission for industry, science and technology have alerted Member States to the dangers of relying on the national perspective. European industry must take full advantage of the continental size of the common market if it is to be able to meet the new challenges in new information technologies, biotechnology, etc. on equal terms with its main competitors. Research and the effective dissemination of research results — in short, greater osmosis between research and industry — will play a central role between now and the end of the 1980s.

The Community's common research policy is still in its infancy, mainly because the Treaties setting up the three European Communities provide very different legal bases for sectoral and general research policy. The Council recognized in a 1974 Resolution that the continued development of a joint policy on science and technology was absolutely necessary.

The first framework programme for the years 1984 to 1987 was adopted by the Community in 1983; it sets out the common strategy in the field of research and

(1) The following paragraphs are largely taken from the booklet 'Vademecum of contract research', Office for Official Publications of the European Communities, Luxembourg, 1984.

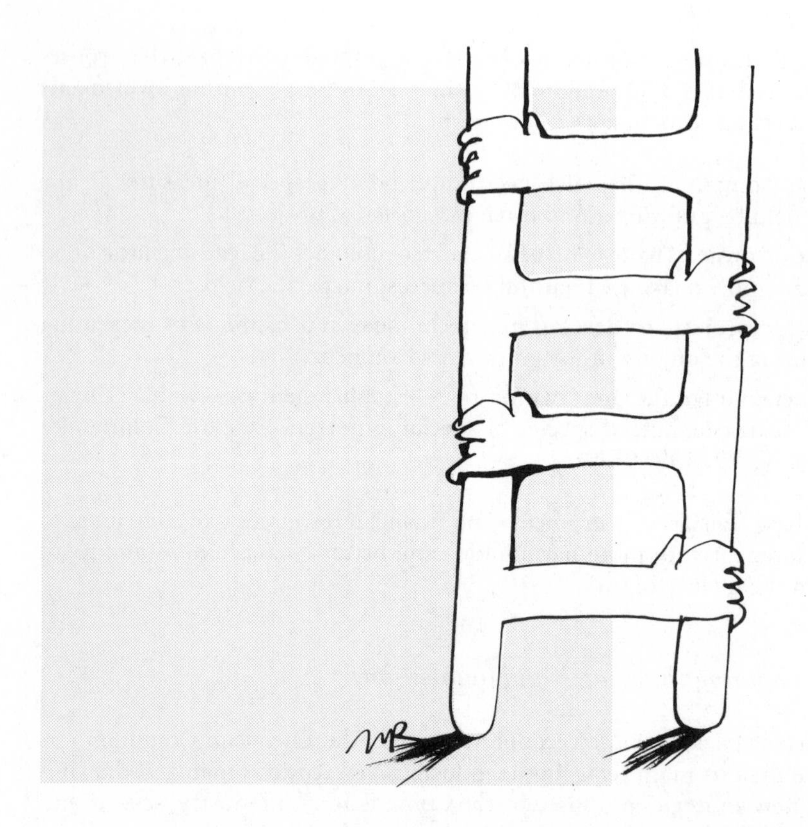

technology and the scientific and technical objectives to be attained at Community level. It also contains the selection criteria for Community activities and defines the priorities. The Community thus has for the first time a true planning instrument in this area of activity.

The common research policy thus established aims to improve the effectiveness of research in the member countries through judicious use of available funds and by concentrating on priority research and development areas. Medium- and long-term research will be possible which individual member countries could not now carry out alone because of its heavy demand on financial and human resources.

Thanks to international cooperation, the common research policy will also facilitate the work of small teams of researchers and make it easier to obtain the desired results. While preventing duplication of effort in member countries, it constitutes an instrument of economic alignment and European integration. Finally, Community research increases European potential for innovation and thus reinforces the Community's economic competitiveness at world level.

The scientific and technical objectives set for the period 1984-87 are as follows:

(i) to promote agricultural competitiveness;

(ii) to promote industrial competitiveness (fewer barriers, new techniques and new products);

(iii) to reinforce Europe's technological base and to improve European industry's international competitiveness in the field of information technology through the Esprit-programme;

(iv) to improve the management of raw materials;

(v) to improve the management of energy resources (nuclear fission energy, controlled thermonuclear fusion, renewable energy sources, rational use of energy);

(vi) to step up development aid;

(vii) to improve living and working conditions;

(viii) to increase the effectiveness of the Community's scientific and technical potential.

In practice, there are essentially four levels of Community research, financed from Community research appropriations at different rates of contribution:

(a) research carried out by the Joint Research Centre (formerly 'direct action')

This research is conducted independently by the Community using its own research staff of some 2 200 persons in the four establishments of the Joint Research Centre: Ispra (Italy), Geel (Belgium), Petten (The Netherlands) and Karlsruhe (Federal Republic of Germany). It is financed entirely out of Community funds, with the nuclear field accounting for about half the expenditure.

(b) contract research (formerly 'indirect action')

Contract research is conducted at universities, research centres or private companies on the basis of cost-sharing contracts with the Community.

This type of research promotion is an important means of coordination. Because of the general and specific selection criteria for Community programmes, it enables that type of project to be launched and backed in the Community which either is not always possible at national level or cannot be carried out by the Joint Research Centre alone in view of the objectives involved. It also provides an opportunity to make use of the research teams and laboratories available in the Member States and to put together the best teams. It is thus extremely important as a stimulus for strong research teams in the Community and therefore as a means of strengthening technological competitiveness in Europe. The Community generally provides 50% of the funds required to finance.

The JET (Joint European Torus) fusion experiment set up at Culham (United Kingdom) and in operation since 1983 is a special case. JET is organized in the form of a 'joint undertaking' under the terms of the Euratom Treaty and is largely autonomous; 80% of its cost is met from the Community budget.

(c) Coordination of research activities (formerly 'concerted action')

The scope of this programme of scientific projects is determined jointly at Community level. However, the individual elements are furnished by the Member States, which wholly finance the projects and are responsible for their implementation. The Commission's role is confined to coordination and the exchange of knowledge.

(d) Cooperative research carried out under the Esprit programme

This research consists of pre-competitive R&D projects in the field of information technology carried out by groups of companies or research institutions from at least two Community countries. The aim is to amplify the combined thrust of R&D activities carried out across the Community and to bring together basic and applied research and university and industrial research.

The projects financed under the Esprit-programme must conform to the priorities laid down in the workplan and are open to industrial and university laboratories and to government research centres active in this field. Half of the research cost is borne by the Community and the remainder by the industrial partners from their own resources.

The programme, which is continually reviewed and subject to further calls for proposals each year, covers five fields:

(i) advanced information processing,
(ii) micro-electronics,
(iii) software technology,
(iv) office automation,
(v) computer integrated manufacturing.

In addition to the common research policy proper, the Community is also taking more direct action to promote industrial innovation.[1] These measures are principally designed to improve the competitiveness of Community industry by promoting the development of new technologies and a favourable European framework for industrial innovation. In addition to aid for demonstration projects in the energy and environmental fields (described above), the Community provides assistance under a multiannual EDP programme and contributes to the transnational development of the infrastructure needed to assist innovation and the transfer of technologies.

More generally, the Community also contributes to the dissemination of information in a number of ways: providing access to research results, commercial intelligence, legal and administrative requirements, business partnerships and contract tenders. The main services are: Euronet-Diane, Euro-Abstracts, Euronews, Industrial Innovation, TED (Tenders Electronic Daily) and the Business Cooperation Centre. All these advanced information services are part of the Community's industrial innovation strategy.

---

(1) For more details, see the booklet 'Industrial innovation: a guide to Community action, services and funding', Office for Official Publications of the European Communities, Luxembourg, 1984.

J — European Investment Bank (EIB)

The European Investment Bank (EIB) was set up by the Treaty of Rome establishing the European Economic Community, which came into force on 1 January 1958.

The EIB is an independent non-profit-making Community institution; its task, as defined in Article 130 of the Treaty of Rome, is to contribute to the balanced development of the Community.

The Bank raises most of its resources on capital markets within and outside the Community and on international markets.

With these resources, it grants long-term loans or gives guarantees to undertakings, public authorities or financial institutions.

The economic policy objectives which the projects financed from the Bank's own resources must meet in the Community are laid down in Article 130 of the Treaty of Rome. In practice, the Bank's funds are used to finance:

(i) investments that contribute to the economic development of the less-developed regions: in 1983, approximately two thirds of the Bank's lending was for investment projects contributing to regional development. These loans went to Italy (half of regional loans), France (15%), Greece (12.8%), the United Kingdom (12.7%), Ireland (8.3%) and, in smaller amounts, Denmark and the Federal Republic of Germany. This aid is concentrated in the regions with priority status for Community regional policy purposes or in regions with the worst unemployment and the lowest per capita GDP;

(ii) investment projects of common interest to several Member States or to the Community as a whole, known as projects of common Community interest:
   (a) which contribute to the economic integration of the Community (communications infrastructures, technical and economic cooperation, etc.),
   (b) or which serve such Community objectives as the protection of the environment, the introduction of advanced technologies and especially more diversified and secure energy supplies (development of domestic resources, rational use and conservation of energy, diversification of imports);

(iii) investment projects for modernizing or converting undertakings or for developing new activities.

The EIB ist thus active in all sectors of the economy. It finances public infrastructures and investment projects in such branches as energy, communications, industry, agriculture and the services sector. In 1983, for example, EIB financing in the Community broke down as follows: energy; 33% of loans; communications, 25%; industry and services, 25%; and infrastructures, 17%. While the Bank's activity covers a wide range of sectors, loans are granted only for investment projects that

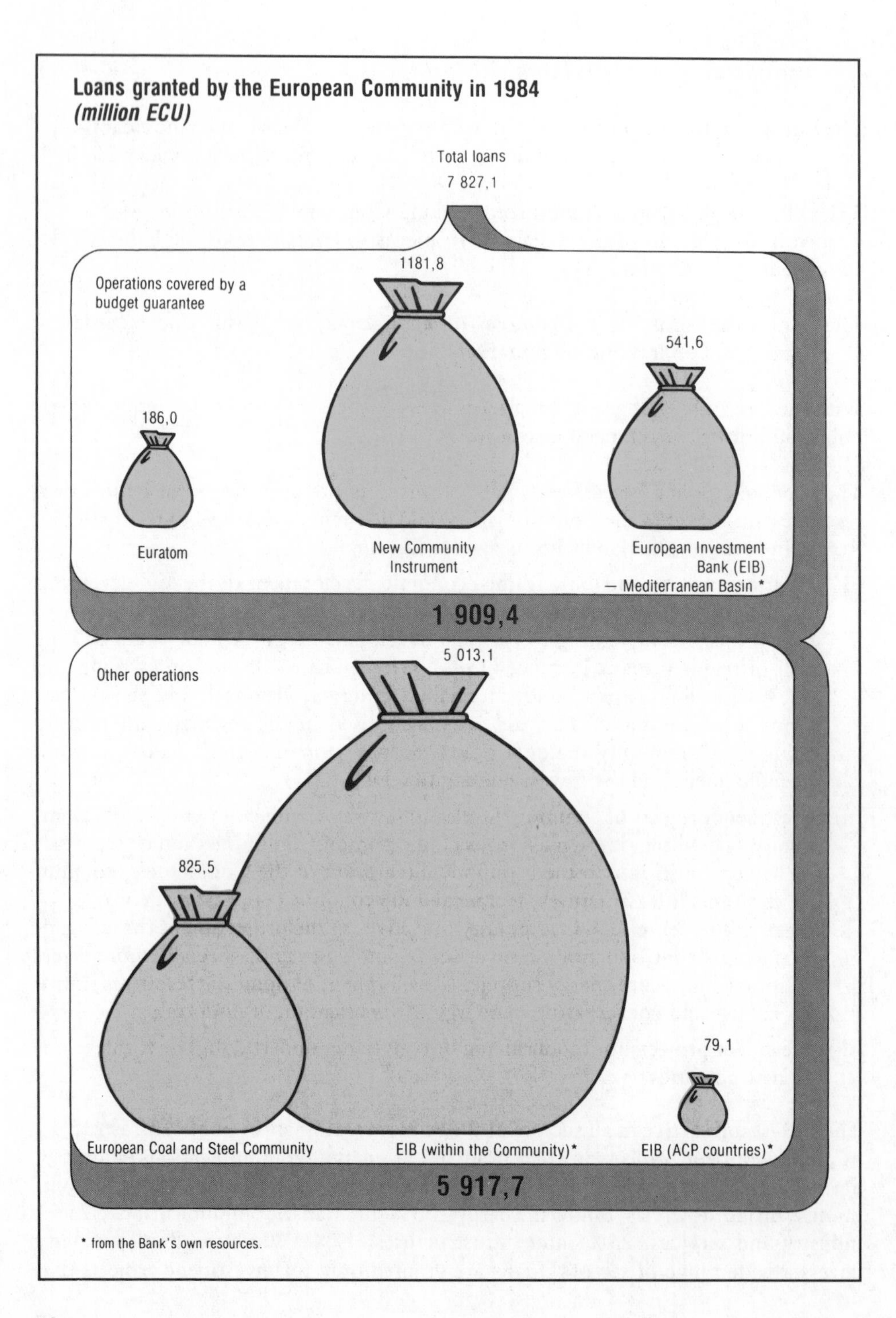
Loans granted by the European Community in 1984
(million ECU)
Total loans
7 827,1
Operations covered by a budget guarantee
186,0
Euratom
1181,8
New Community Instrument
541,6
European Investment Bank (EIB) — Mediterranean Basin *
1 909,4
Other operations
825,5
European Coal and Steel Community
5 013,1
EIB (within the Community)*
79,1
EIB (ACP countries)*
5 917,7
* from the Bank's own resources.

contribute directly or indirectly to increasing economic productivity in general. This means that the economic grounds for projects and their effects on employment are examined closely.

EIB loans are not conditional on the nationality or legal status of the borrower, although projects eligible for EIB financing must normally be carried out in the European territories of Member States.

The Bank Statute does, however, provide that loans may be granted for projects outside the Community with the special permission of the Board of Governors. Permission is given on an *ad hoc* basis for individual loans for investment projects outside European territories of the Member States that are of particular interest to the Community, e.g. for its energy supply; and permission is given on a comprehensive basis for a stated amount of lending in respect of a given country or group of countries under association or cooperation agreements between the Community and certain non-member or applicant countries.

The Bank's theatre of operations now covers 64 countries in Africa, the Caribbean and the Pacific, Portugal and Spain, Turkey and Yugoslavia, the Maghreb countries (Algeria, Morocco and Tunisia), the Mashreq countries (Egypt, Jordan, Lebanon and Syria), Israel, Cyprus and Malta. In addition to loans from its own resources, the Bank furnishes most of these countries with concessionary aid drawn from budgetary funds and managed on behalf of the Community. Such operations are accounted for off balance sheet in the Bank's Special Section.

The Bank also acts as agent in appraising and administering Euratom loans approved by the Commission.

Since 1979 it has also, acting as agent for the Community, been granting loans from the resources of the New Community Instrument for borrowing and lending (NCI) to finance projects approved as eligible by the Commission.

K — New Community Instrument for borrowing and lending (NCI)

It was in 1978 that the Council of the European Communities first decided to set alongside the Community's existing financial institutions and bodies, a new Community instrument for borrowing and lending (NCI). The general aim of this instrument is to finance, in the form of loans, investment projects which contribute to greater convergence and integration of the economic policies of the Member States (Council Decision 78/870/EEC).

To this end, the Commission is empowered by the Council to contract loans on behalf of the Community the proceeds of which are lent to finance investment projects on Community territory. The projects must serve priority Community objectives in the energy, industrial and infrastructure sectors, account being taken *inter alia* of their regional impact and the need to combat unemployment.

With the introduction of the NCI, the Community increased its borrowing capacity by widening its scope for raising resources; the NCI provides a broader and more diversified guarantee for Community lending operations, NCI borrowings being guaranteed by the general budget of the European Communities.

The NCI is thus a general instrument for reviving investment, particularly in industry (especially small business), the development of energy resources, energy conservation and infrastructures linked to productive activities contributing to regional development and being of Community interest.

The maximum amounts of borrowings authorized have been: in 1978, 1 000 million ECU (Decision 78/870/EEC); in 1982, 1 000 million ECU (Decision 82/169/EEC); in 1983, 3 000 million ECU (Decision 83/200/EEC).

Borrowings are activated tranche by tranche. The Council, acting unanimously on a proposal from the Commission and after consulting the European Parliament, authorizes each tranche and lays down the guidelines for the eligibility of projects.

The EIB grants and administers loans under the NCI in the name, for the account and at the risk of the Community.

Loan applications are transmitted simultaneously to the Commission and to the Bank; the Commission decides whether the projects proposed are eligible; the Bank takes the grant decisions and sets the terms of loans in accordance with the procedures laid down by its statute and its usual criteria. Finally, the financing agreements are signed by the Commission and the Bank.

The growth of the Community's financial instruments for structural purposes (1973-83)

1. Table 1 shows how the financial commitments of the Community instruments for a structural purpose have grown between 1973 and 1983.

Sectoral aids (EAGGF Guidance Section, ECSC, specific energy measures) expanded at the end of the period after remaining at much the same level from 1973 to 1978. Aid from the EAGGF Guidance Section increased over those five years by less than 50% — a decline in real terms, as consumer prices rose by over 70% during the same period. With the large increases of 1979 and 1983, EAGGF aid in real terms was some 97% higher in 1983 than in 1973 (i.e. an average annual increase of 7%).

ECSC grants from its budget (interest subsidies, redeployment aid, aid for coking coal and, since 1981, social aid) increased appreciably in 1981 with the introduction of special measures aimed at retraining and re-employing workers in the steel industry.

After increasing rapidly in 1974 and 1975, the level of ECSC lending has fluctuated fairly widely without reaching the levels recorded in those two years. Euratom loans increased substantially in the first five years following their introduction in 1977; since then, they have stabilized at some 360 million ECU per year. The budgetary resources allocated by the Community to other specific measures in the energy field, in particular demonstration projects, have stabilized in recent years at an annual level of between 70 and 80 million ECU.

Horizontal measures, in particular regional and social measures, have expanded very rapidly. The Regional Fund has grown the fastest, with an average annual increase of 31% in its commitments since it was set up in 1975. Over the same period, the Social Fund has expanded by 24% per year on average. Since 1973, aid from the Social Fund has increased elevenfold. EIB operations expanded steadily between 1973 and 1983, by some 21% per year.

The other horizontal lending instrument, the NCI, has also grown considerably; since it was set up in 1979, its lending volume has increased by 45% per year on average. Finally, the financial aid granted in connection with the Community's research activities has increased fivefold in the last 10 years, reaching 463 million ECU in 1983.

2. Table 2 shows all Community grants and loans for structural purposes in absolute figures, as a percentage of GDP, as a percentage of the Community budget (for grants) and as a percentage of the Community's net public sector borrowing requirement (for loans).

Grants for structural purposes totalled 407 million ECU in 1973 and 5 900 million ECU in 1983 — a striking increase of some 30% per year. The growth rate was particularly high in two years of the period: 56% from 1974 to 1975 (mainly owing to the inception of the Regional Fund) and 62% from 1978 to 1979 (mainly owing to increased endowments for the Regional and Social Funds and the introduction of EMS interest subsidies).

Grants for structural purposes came to almost 22 ECU per head of population in the Community in 1983, compared with 2 ECU in 1973. They absorbed 9% of the Community budget in 1973 and 22% in 1983, having represented a fairly stable share of just under 14% from 1974 to 1978. Grants for structural purposes represented only 0.05% of Community GDP in 1973; this percentage increased almost fivefold to 0.23% in 1983.

Total loans for structural purposes increased from 945 million ECU in 1973 to 6 600 million ECU in 1983, an annual increase of some 21%. These loans represented 3.7 ECU per head of population in 1973 and 24.3 ECU in 1983. As a percentage of GDP, the loans increased from 0.11% in 1973 to 0.26% in 1983.

As the net public sector borrowing requirement of the Community increased faster than Community lending between 1973 and 1975, the percentage share of these loans in the borrowing requirement fell from 16% in 1973 to 3% in 1975; since 1976, it has remained stable at about 5%.

As the figures show, most of the Community's financial instruments have developed rapidly in recent years. The amounts involved are still small in relation to national aggregates so that there is a permanent need to make them more effective.

TABLE I

Community grants and loans for structural purposes, by instrument, 1973–83

(in million ECU)

	Grants								Loans				
	Agricultural Fund Guidance	Social Fund	Regional Fund	European Monetary System + earthquake interest subsidies	Energy demonstration projets	Research and development (a)	European Coal and Steel Community budget (a)	Total budget aid (b)	European Investment Bank (c)	European Coal and Steel Community	Euratom	New Community Instrument (c)	Total loans
1973	183.6	167.7	–	–	–	–	55.2	407.0	652.5	292.2	–	–	944.7
1974	254.8	234.7	–	–	–	92.5	54.0	636.0	846.4	410.2	–	–	1256.6
1975	247.2	330.4	249.90	–	38.9	127.3	47.7	993.7	971.6	1098.1	–	–	2015.7
1976	310.4	364.4	387.90	–	38.5	147.0	41.0	1289.2	1086.0	1081.0	–	–	2167.0
1977	312.7	499.0	385.80	–	20.0	209.4	50.8	1477.7	1352.6	989.6	96.90	–	2439.1
1978	269.2	568.3	561.40	–	36.7	242.6	96.9	1775.1	1966.5	797.7	70.30	–	2834.5
1979	507.3	774.5	970.40	200.0	70.1	237.7	120.3	2880.3	2141.8	675.8	152.50	277.0	3347.1
1980	627.7	1014.2	1126.40	197.0	78.1	284.3	131.9	3456.6	2702.3	1020.3	171.50	197.6	4091.7
1981	725.4	1003.8	1708.96	193.2	59.2	351.7	210.0	4252.4	2516.6	387.6	364.29	539.8	3808.3
1982	783.0	1532.0	1895.00	212.7	79.8	389.2	264.2	5155.9	3453.2	668.9	361.60	791.0	5274.7
1983	943.7	1876.1	2121.20	214.4	82.0	462.6	234.0	5934.1	4255.7	776.6	366.50	1211.8	6610.6

(a) ECSC research aid is included under 'Research and development'.
(b) Excluding supplementary measures and special measures in favour of the United Kingdom and the Federal Republic of Germany:
1980 : UK = 194 million ECU — 1982 : UK = 1 804 million ECU.
1981 : UK = 1 244 million ECU — 1983 : UK = 1 400 million ECU — FR of Germany = 273 million ECU.
(c) Including special loans following earthquakes: Southern Italy (1981-83); Greece (1982).

TABLE 2

Total Community grants and loans for structural purposes [1] in absolute figures, as a percentage of the Community budget or of the net public sector borrowing requirement (PSBR) of the Community and as a percentage of Community GDP, 1973–83

	Grants				Loans			
	Million ECU	per capita	% of Community budget	% of Community GDP	Million ECU	ECU per capita	% of net PSBR of the Community	% of Community GDP
1973	407.0	1.6	9	0.05	944.7	3.7	16	0.11
1974	636.0	2.5	11	0.06	1256.6	4.9	8	0.13
1975	993.7	3.9	14	0.09	2015.7	7.8	3	0.18
1976	1289.2	5.0	14	0.10	2167.0	8.4	5	0.17
1977	1477.7	5.3	14	0.10	2439.1	9.0	5	0.17
1978	1775.1	6.9	14	0.11	2834.5	10.9	5	0.18
1979	2880.3	11.1	19	0.16	3347.1	12.8	5	0.19
1980	3456.6	13.3	20	0.17	4091.7	15.7	6	0.21
1981	4252.4	15.7	21	0.19	3808.3	14.0	3	0.17
1982	5155.9	19.0	22	0.21	5274.7	19.3	4	0.22
1983	5934.1	21.7	22	0.23	6610.6	24.3	5	0.26

[1] The breakdown by financial instrument is shown in Table 1 on the previous page.

The Commission would like to see this improvement achieved through increased Community conditionality of financial aid, by focusing the effort on the most serious problems, by dovetailing the aims and operation of the various Community instruments and by coordinating Community and national measures, so that Community action genuinely augments the national effort.

Part 2: Financial aid operations from the viewpoint of the recipients

This part of the booklet is essentially a summary of the third part, in which the working of the financial instruments is described in greater detail under the headings 'Eligibility and selection criteria', 'Financial provisions' and 'Procedural questions'. Since it is rather difficult for a potential beneficiary to go through all the different schemes, an attempt is made in this part to indicate which instruments could be of interest to him, that is to say this second part is intended as a quick reference guide for the questions which will be asked by potential beneficiaries of Community assistance:

(i) whether they are likely to qualify for assistance,

(ii) how to submit an application for assistance,

(iii) when they will be paid (if assistance has been agreed upon).

Chapter I in this part deals with the types of economic activities qualifying for financial assistance. Chapter II answers questions about application procedures and the timing of applications. Chapter III is concerned with the scheduling of aids and with the recipients.

Chapter I — Categories of economic activity eligible for Community assistance

The Community's financial instruments cover a very wide range of economic activities, but the assistance provided falls into the following main categories:

(i) assistance for investment, covering productive investment, infrastructure investment and energy;[1]

(ii) assistance facilitating occupational and geographical mobility, and employment subsidies;

(iii) aid for exploiting potential for internally generated development;

(iv) financial contributions to research and the dissemination of knowledge.

---

(1) For energy, the distinction between assistance for productive and for infrastructure schemes is particularly difficult to establish and definitions vary according to Member States. For this reason energy is taken as a separate category.

A — Assistance for investment

The various schemes covering assistance for investment are shown in Table 1. The first column indicates the coverage of the different schemes, i.e. the activity sector for productive investment, the type of infrastructure investment and the type of energy measure. The second column shows which instrument relates to a particular activity; it shows that only the Regional Fund, the EIB, the NCI and conversion aids cover all sectors. The figures in brackets after the instruments refer to the tables in Part 3, in which the instruments are described in greater detail, e.g. EIB (X.1) shows that the scheme is listed as the first in Table X. The last column shows the geographical scope of the measure and mentions additional sectoral restrictions if they are of importance.

For productive investment, some schemes are specific to particular economic activities: agriculture, agricultural products, fisheries, forestry, rural tourism, and coal and steel industries. Only the EIB, the NCI, the Regional Fund and the ECSC conversion aids are of general scope.

For infrastructural investment, the situation is the same. Some measures apply to specific types of infrastructure only; these are rural infrastructure, water engineering schemes for agriculture, forestry, vocational training centres, industrial and urban sites, housing and infrastructure linked to rural tourism. On the other hand, the EIB, the Regional Fund and the NCI cover a broad range of infrastructure investments, including the specific categories mentioned above except that agricultural improvements are excluded from Regional Fund aid, and there is a list of infrastruc-

TABLE 1

Community financial assistance to productive investment, infrastructure investment and energy[1]

A. Contributions to productive investment (excluding energy)

Coverage of scheme	Scheme [2]	Geographical scope and any additional sectoral restrictions
1. All sectors [1]	EIB (X)	All regions, particularly less-favoured regions in the case of the EIB
2. All sectors except agriculture, forestry, fisheries	Regional Fund (IV.2 to 4)	ERDF regions
	EIB (X.2), NCI (X.I)	
	ECSC (V.2 + 5)	Areas affected by the decline in coal and steel industry employment
	Environment (VIII.1 + 2)	Demonstration of new 'clean' technologies and measuring techniques.

Coverage of scheme	Scheme [2]	Geographical scope and any additional sectoral restrictions
3. Agriculture	EAGGF Guidance (certain indirect measures)	cf. Table I in Part 3
4. Agricultural and fishery products (processing and marketing)	EAGGF Guidance (I.1)	All regions; investments at retail level are excluded
5. Fisheries	Fishery measures (II.1 to 4)	All fishing areas; fishing and aquaculture
6. Forestry	EAGGF Guidance (I.3 and I.27)	Italian, French and Greek Mediterranean forests
7. Coal and steel industries	ECSC (V.1 + 4)	All regions with coal or steel enterprises

B. Contributions to infrastructure investment (excluding energy)

Coverage of scheme	Scheme [2]	Geographical scope and any eligibility restrictions
8. All eligible infrastructure, in particular transport, telecommunications, water treatment and supply, housing schemes, environmental protection and the specific categories 9 to 15 below	Regional Fund (IV.2 and 4) EIB (X), NCI (XI)	ERDF regions; certain infrastructure categories excluded (list of exclusions) All regions
9. Rural infrastructure, in particular farm access, roads, electricity, drinking water, purification of water	EAGGF Guidance (I.2, 5, 6, 19, 22, 24, 26, 27) Regional Fund (IV.2 + 4)	cf. Table I in Part 3 Less favoured regions of Directive 75/268 if they are also ERDF regions
10. Water engineering schemes for agriculture	EAGGF Guidance (I.5, 7, 13, 14, 15, 16, 26, 27)	cf. Table I in Part 3
11. Forestry	EAGGF Guidance (I.3)	Italian, French and Greek Mediterranean forests
12. Vocational training centres	Social Fund (III.7) ECSC (V.1)	ESF regions; depreciation cost only
13. Industrial sites	ECSC (V.3 + 6)	Areas affected by the decline in coal and steel industry employment (ECSC employment areas)
14. Housing	ECSC (V.3)	All regions with coal or steel enterprises
15. Transport infrastructure	Transport infrastructure (VII)	All regions Projects contributing to the elimination of bottlenecks or to the improvement of links between Member States.

C. Contributions to investment in the energy sector

Coverage scheme	Scheme [2]	Geographical scope and any eligibility restrictions
16. General schemes that include energy	Regional Fund (IV.2 to 5)	ERDF regions
	EIB (X), NCI (XI)	All regions
17. Specific energy measures	Euratom loans (VI.1)	cf. Table VI in Part 3. All regions
	Technological development in the hydrocarbons sector (VI.2)	
	Demonstration projects in the energy sector (VI.3 + 4)	All regions, limited to demonstration projects
	Regional Fund (specific Community measure)	Mezzogiorno, Greek Islands (except Salamis)

[1] For energy, the distinction between contributions for productive and for infrastructure schemes is particularly difficult to establish and definitions vary according to Member States. For this reason, energy is taken as a separate category.
[2] The numbers following the scheme refer to the table in Part 3 and the number of the scheme in that table, e.g. EIB (X.1) shows that the scheme is listed as the first in Table X.
[3] Including agriculture, forestry, fisheries, industry services, tourism and the craft sector.
[4] The indirect measures of the EAGGF Guidance Section are not dealt with in detail in this booklet, cf. Part 3, Chapter 1 B.
[5] There is no exhaustive list of eligible infrastructure categories for any Community instrument. The range listed below covers the infrastructure categories for which eligibility is well established. Other types of infrastructure might be considered in particular circumstances and according to criteria specific to each scheme. For the Regional Fund, there is a list excludiing certain categories of infrastructure.

ture categories which the Regional Fund may not assist (educational establishments, hospitals, administrative buildings, housing etc.).

Similarly, there are specific energy schemes for industrial production of electricity in nuclear power stations and industrial fuel cycle installations, in the hydrocarbons sector, for energy saving and for the development of new sources of energy. As in the case of infrastructure investments, general schemes exist under the Regional Fund, the EIB and the NCI covering all energy projects designed to develop Community resources in the fields of hydroelectricity, geothermal energy, nuclear energy, oil and natural gas deposits, solid fuels, alternative energy sources, energy saving and import diversification projects e.g. for gaslines or power stations to run on imported coal.

B — Aids facilitating occupational and geographical mobility

These types of aid cover all Social Fund operations and the ECSV redeployment aids, the list is given in Table 2.

TABLE 2

Aids facilitating occupational and geographical mobility; employment subsidies

A. Aids facilitating occupational and geographical mobility

Coverage of scheme	Scheme
1. Vocational training in off-the-job public or private training centres and workshops, and in the undertaking; instructors' training	Social Fund (III.) ECSC (V.6 and 7)
2. Resettlement and integration into new social and working environment	Social Fund (III.) ECSC (V.6 and 7)
3. Job adjustment and functional rehabilitation of handicapped persons	Social Fund (III.)
4. Income maintenance for: – persons undergoing vocational training – ECSC workers	Social Fund (III.) ECSC (V.6 and 7)

B. Employment subsidies

Coverage of scheme	Scheme
5. Recruitment and employment aid for: (i) young people below 25 years of age (ii) the long-term unemployed	Social Fund (III.7)

Among aids to facilitate occupational mobility, vocational training is the type of measure given the greatest assistance. This type of action may cover Community assistance for maintaining the income levels of persons undergoing vocational training and — in the case of the vocational integration of handicapped persons for job adjustment.

Employment aids are restricted to aid for recruitment to additional permanent jobs or for employment in projects designed to create additional jobs which fulfil a public need. These aids may benefit either young people below the age of 25 or the long-term unemployed.

C — Aid for exploiting the potential for internally generated development of regions

Aid for exploiting internally generated development potential is not yet large, but it is a new and original form of Community assistance differing from traditional investment aids.

The Community first co-financed projects in this field when the specific regional development measures were introduced for the first time in 1980 for a period of five years and were then widened and given more generous funding in 1984 for a further five-year period (see Part 3, Chapter IV, last section). The types of aid covered by these specific measures include, in addition to investment, provision of resources and services which small and medium-sized firms require to extend their activities (sectoral analyses, management or organizational advice, economic promotion, common services, etc.), the promotion of innovation in industry and services, and the development of craft industries and tourism. These types of aid meet special regional needs and are applied only in certain areas (see end of Chapter IV in Part 3).

Since the beginning of 1985, the Community has extended this type of aid to all ERDF regions through the new Regional Fund Regulation. The measures provided for are similar to those described above and consist in making available to firms in industry and the craft and tourism sectors facilities to enable them to expand their activities and to gain access to new technologies and to the capital market. These measures include aid for surveys, aid for applied research designed to foster the internal generation of regional development, and aid for:

(i) technology transfers,

(ii) sectoral studies,

(iii) access to management and organizational advice,

(iv) the setting up of common services,

(v) the promotion of tourism and coordinated management of accomodation, and

(vi) measures to facilitate firms' access to the capital market.

Finally, the Community may contribute, under the same series of measures, to public expenditure on the planning, technical preparation and implementation of Regional Fund operations (see Table IV in Part 3). This aid constitutes a type of technical assistance.

D — Financial contributions to research activities and the dissemination of knowledge

In addition to the research activities carried out by the Community's own staff in 'Joint Research Centre' establishments, the Community helps to provide financial backing for research projects carried out by universities, research centres and private companies or public undertakings on the basis of cost-sharing contracts concluded with the Community (see Table IX-A in Part 3).

The Community also provides access to information through a range of services: among other things it disseminates research results, commercial intelligence and statutory and administrative requirements. In some cases, the Community may help to finance such measures (see Table IX-B in Part 3).

Chapter II — Procedures and timetable for submission of applications

Submission Procedures

Investors or responsible bodies apply for financial assistance in one of the following ways:

(i) they may apply direct to the Commission or the EIB;

(ii) they may apply to the Commission only through the Member State concerned and with its approval;

(iii) only Member States may submit applications for assistance; these are drawn up by the investors or responsible bodies;

(iv) applications are sent to the Member State concerned, which takes all necessary decisions and is reimbursed by the Community; thus, investors or responsible bodies benefit only indirectly from the Community assistance.

The first and most direct way of submitting applications may be used for ECSC industrial loans (V.1), EIB loans (X.1-3), NCI loans (XI), specific energy measures (VI.1-4) and environment measures (VIII.1-2) and measures relating to research and innovation (IX-A and IX-B).

The method of submitting applications through Member States and with their approval applies to direct measures under the EAGGF Guidance Section (I.1-7) and in the fishery sector (II.1), to ECSC conversion loans (V.2) and to one of the specific measures in the environmental field (VIII.3). All applications to the Social Fund (III.1-7), to the Regional Fund (IV.1-5) and in respect of transport infrastructure (VII) are submitted to the Commission by the Member State in question.

Indirect measures under the EAGGF Guidance Section (I.8-38) and in the fishery sector (II.2-4) and the Regional Fund programmes (IV.2-3) are administered by the Member States, which may receive advances on annual expenditure and are reimbursed by the Commission on presentation of documents proving the expenditure has been incurred.

In the case of specific measures and programmes under the Regional Fund, the Commission's payment is not necessarily a reimbursement of expenditure incurred by the Member State but may be an additional allocation to the investor; the national authorities may sometimes not be involved at all in certain specific aid categories.

Timing of submission

For some measures there is no fixed date by which applications must be submitted, for others there is a closing date. The closing date may be fixed or may vary, as laid down in Commission communications.

A fixed closing date is laid down for Regulations (EEC) No 355/77 and No 2908/83 in the case of the EAGGF Guidance Section and for Social Fund measures. The closing date for Regulation 355/77 is 1 May of the year of commitment of expenditure; the dates for Regulation 2908/83 are 31 March and 31 October of each year. For Social Fund measures, the closing date is 21 October of the year preceding the operations.

For direct measures under the EAGGF Guidance Section applications must be submitted before work commences; for Social Fund measures they must be submitted before an operation is completed.

The Commission publishes in the *Official Journal of the European Communities* the closing dates for ECSC interest subsidies on industrial loans (IV.1 + 4), ECSC research aid (V.9), specific energy measures other than Euratom loans (VI.2-4), specific environmental measures (VIII.1-2) and most measures relating to research and innovation (IX-A and IX-B).

Chapter III — Scheduling of aids; recipients

Loans and interest subsidies are administered in accordance with normal banking practice. In the case of global loans, the Commission or the EIB makes payments to financial intermediaries which distribute them to the final beneficiaries (e.g. small or medium-sized firms).

For direct measures under the EAGGF Guidance Section, payments are made through agencies appointed by the Member State concerned. In the case of measures under Regulations (EEC) No 355/77 and No 2908/83, assistance is granted in successive instalments as work progresses and on submission of documentary evidence to the Commission. For other direct measures, advances of up to 80% of the total Community contribution may be made on annual expenditure on a project.

In the case of Social Fund and the Regional Fund, payments are effected through the Member States concerned. Amounts are distributed within Member States according to internal rules which vary from one country to another. The Commission allocates appropriations to the Member States according to uniform rules, which are different for the two Funds.

(a) In the case of the Social Fund, once an application connected with employment policy measures is approved, an advance of 50% of the assistance granted is paid on the date scheduled for the commencement of the measures. When an application in respect of specific measures is approved, an initial advance of 30% of the aid granted is paid. A second advance of 30% may be paid as soon as the Member State concerned certifies that half the operation has been carried out in accordance with the conditions laid down in the approval decision. The balance is paid after a detailed report on the content, results and financial aspects of the operation has been received.

(b) In the case of the Regional Fund, two advances are made before the balance is paid: the first, not exceeding 40%, at the beginning of the operations; the second as soon as half the first advance has been spent. The two advances may not together exceed 80% of the total amount committed. The balance is paid on completion of the operations. In the case of jointly financed programmes, payments are made concomitantly with progress on the planned annual segments; in the case of aid for projects, the system of advance payments applies to the total amount of Fund assistance for each project.

For the specific measures in the fields of energy (other than Euratom loans), the environment and research and development activities, all the arrangements relating to the scheduling and timing of payments are laid down in the contracts concluded between the Commission and the promoter.

Part 3: The financial instruments and how they operate

This part of the booklet provides technical information on the financial instruments at present serving of Community's structural policy. It is divided into 12 chapters:

I — EAGGF Guidance Section

II — Measures to improve fishery structures

III — European Social Fund

IV — European Regional Development Fund

V — ECSC financial activities

VI — Specific measures for the energy sector

VII — Special aid for transport infrastructure

VIII — Community action on the environment

IX — Measures relating to research and innovation

X — European Investment Bank (EIB) loans

XI — New Community Instrument (NCI) loans

XII — Special measures

Each chapter contains: a sumary table showing the different financial measures covered by the instrument; the instrument's general objective and, if applicable, its main subdivisions; information on the eligibility and selection criteria; the financing rules, including the rate of Community participation and procedures, including the submission of applications.

Where the money goes
Distribution of grants and loans for structural purposes, 1983

Grants *(in million ECU)*

Country	Agricultural Fund (EAGGF) Guidance	Social Fund	Regional Fund	European Monetary System and earthquake interest rebates	Total General European Community Budget	European Coal and Steel Community Budget (b)	Total
I	232,4	534,0	818,9	151,8	1 737,1	2,0	1 739,1
UK (a)	157,3	558,0	459,9	—	1 175,2	101,2	1 276,4
IRL	101,4	182,0	106,5	60,8	450,7	0,1	450,8
GR	85,1	114,0	355,4	1,8	556,3	—	556,3
Group A	576,2	1 388,0	1 740,7	214,4	3 919,3	103,3	4 022,6
D	113,0	110,6	43,8	—	267,4	53,0	320,4
F	186,6	277,6	285,4	—	749,6	10,8	760,4
NL	29,3	24,2	20,1	—	73,6	1,2	74,8
B	16,0	32,7	8,9	—	57,6	10,9	68,5
L	1,5	0,9	0,0	—	2,4	0,2	2,6
DK	21,1	42,1	22,4	—	85,6	1,6	87,2
Group B	367,5	488,1	380,6	—	1 236,2	77,7	1 313,9
CEE 10	943,7	1 876,1	2 121,2	214,4	5 155,5	181,0	5 336,4

Loans *(in millions of ECU)*

Country	European Investment Bank (c)	European Coal and Steel Community	Euratom	New Community Instrument (c)	Total
I	1 945,7	32,0	89,2	665,4	2 732,3
UK (a)	591,3	270,0	45,6	100,1	1 007,0
IRL	234,6	4,3	—	69,4	308,3
GR	364,3	0,5	—	85,3	450,1
Group A	3 135,9	306,8	134,8	920,2	4 497,7
D	152,2	149,0	—	—	301,2
F	707,9	278,0	199,4	186,2	1 371,5
NL	—	39,0	—	—	39,0
B	—	3,8	32,3	—	36,1
L	—	0,0	—	—	0,0
DK	259,7	0,0	—	105,4	365,1
Group B	1 119,8	469,8	231,7	291,6	2 112,9
CEE 10	4 255,7	776,6	366,5	1 211,8	6 610,6

(a) Exluding special and supplementary measures, i. e. U. K. = 1 399.6 Million ECU and Germany = 272,5 Million ECU.
(b) Readaption grants, 'volet social' for the steel industry and coking coal aid only.
(c) Including special earthquake loans in favour of Southern Italy.

Chapter I — EAGGF Guidance Section[1]
(see Table I for list of measures)

Aim

The EAGGF Guidance section represents the structural part of the common agricultural policy and follows its general objectives (as laid down in Article 39 of the EEC Treaty). In addition, the different EAGGF Guidance Section measures have a specific purpose of their own which is generally indicated in the title of the measure.

Main features

The activities of the EAGGF Guidance Section are divided into direct measures and indirect measures. In the case of direct measures, aid is granted for private or public investment projects. In the case of indirect measures, the Fund reimburses Member States for expenditure incurred for certain measures.

A further important distinction lies in the areas of assistance. Since it was set up, the Guidance Section has concentrated on the following fields:

(i) the structural improvement of farms,

(ii) the improvement of rural infrastructure, and

(iii) the improvement of marketing and processing of agricultural and fishery products.

In addition, there are a number of measures which do not fall or fall only partly under these three headings.

A. Direct measures

Table I contains a list of the direct financial aid measures for private and public investors in respect of investment projects or programmes. The largest in volume terms is the measure to improve the processing and marketing of agricultural and fishery products.

Improving the processing and marketing of agricultural and fishery products (Regulation (EEC) No 355/77 as amended by Regulation (EEC) No 1932/84)

Eligibility and selection criteria

Projects eligible under the Regulation are public, semi-public or private material investment projects in the marketing (but not at retail level) of the products listed in Annex II to the Treaty of Rome or the production of the processed products listed in that annex.

Subject to certain special conditions, projects may relate to the processing of products listed in Annex II to the Treaty into products not listed in that annex or to the marketing of such goods; these projects must provide economic benefits for the producer of the basic agricultural product.

---

[1] Excluding specific measures relating to fishery structures.

In view of the Community's production objectives, certain sectors may be excluded from Community aid or subject to different provisions.

To be eligible, projects must relate to building and/or equipment for:

(a) rationalizing or developing storage, market preparation, preservation, treatment or processing of agricultural products;

(b) improving marketing channels;

(c) better knowledge of the facts relating to prices and their formation on the markets for agricultural products;

(d) testing the technical and economic feasibility of new processing techniques on an industrial scale (pilot projects);

(e) saving energy or removing or recycling industrial residues or waste generated by other eligible facilities;

(f) harvesting primary products of the soil subject to certain conditions laid down in the Regulation (the project must not be eligible for Community aid under Directive 72/159/EEC: equipment forming part of a project for the processing of the products concerned; specific equipment which is indispensable; a first acquisition of equipment the use of which is economically justified).

Projects must form part of specific programmes drawn up by the Member States for the various agricultural and fishery products; they must offer adequate guarantees that they will be profitable and will help to improve the situation of the basic agricultural production sector in question.

Aid from the Fund is primarily for projects fulfilling one or more of the following criteria:

(i) they must help to develop the types of farming encouraged under the common agricultural policy (e. g. new outlets, new products);

(ii) they must lighten the burden on the intervention mechanisms of the common organization of markets;

(iii) they must be in regions experiencing particular difficulty in adjusting to the conditions and economic consequences of the common agricultural policy, or they must benefit such regions;

(iv) they must help to improve marketing channels or to rationalize the processing of products;

(v) they must help to improve the quality or ensure better use of by-products.

Since the volume of applications for aid generally far exceeds the available resources, the Commission has laid down more detailed criteria for selecting projects; these criteria can be used to determine, for each group of agricultural and fishery products, the types of investment which should be given priority and those on which there should be certain restrictions. These selection criteria are published in the Official Journal.

Financial provisions

Assistance from the Fund consists of capital grants not exceeding:

(i) 50% of the investment in the case of projects carried out in the Mezzogiorno, the West of Ireland, Greece (except Greater Athens) and the French overseas departments;

(ii) 35% in the case of projects carried out in certain regions in the south of France (Languedoc-Roussillon and the departments of Vaucluse, Bouches-du-Rhône, Var, Ardèche and Drôme);

(iii) 25% in other regions; this rate may be increased to 30% for projects in regions suffering particular difficulties.

The recipient must provide at least 50% of the cost of the investment; this contribution is reduced to 35% in the case of the regions in the south of France and to 25% in the case of the Mezzogiorno, the West of Ireland, Greece (except for Greater Athens) and the French overseas departments.

The member State concerned must contribute at least 5%.

Finally, the financial conditions are different in the case of harvesting equipment. Aid from the Fund is between 10% and 30% depending on the location of the projects, while the minimum contribution from the recipient varies between 60% and 80%.

Procedures

Aid may be granted to the natural or legal persons, or groups thereof, who are ultimately responsible for the cost of carrying out the project. Applications for aid from the Fund must be submitted through the Member State concerned before 1 May in accordance with the rules laid down in Commission Regulation (EEC) No 219/78 (as amended by Regulation (EEC) No 3397/82); they must have been approved by the competent authorities in the Member State concerned.

Fund aid is payable in instalments as the work progresses, on submission of documentary evidence to the Commission. Payments are made through agencies appointed by the Member State concerned. Payment arrangements are laid down in Commission Regulation (EEC) No 1685/78.

Improvement of public amenities in certain rural areas of France and Italy (Council Regulation (EEC) No 1760/78 as amended by Council Regulation (EEC) No 2003/83)

Eligibility criteria

Under Regulation (EEC) No 1760/78, any public, semi-public or private physical investment project is eligible which relates wholly or in part to:

(i) the provision of electricity or drinking water to villages or parts of villages whose inhabitants are dependent principally on agriculture, and to isolated farmsteads;

(ii) the construction and improvement of farm roads and local roads which are mainly used for agriculture and forestry.

These projects must be included in an outline programme and must be located in the less-favoured areas in Italy or the south of France, namely:

(i) the less-favoured regions within the meaning of Directive 75/268/EEC in Italy and in the south of France, in the regions of Midi-Pyrénées, Languedoc-Roussillon, Provence-Côte d'Azur and Corsica and in the departments of Pyrénées-Atlantiques, Ardèche and Drôme;

(ii) the other areas of the Mezzogiorno.

Projects for which Community aid is provided under other common measures of the EAGGF Guidance Section or through the European Regional Development Fund are not eligible.

Financial provisions

The Fund's participation rate is 40% of the approved investment. The recipient must provide 10% and the Member State concerned at least 20%.

Procedures

Aid may be granted to the natural or legal persons, or groups thereof, who are ultimately responsible for the cost of carrying out the project. Applications for aid from the Fund must be submitted through the Member State concerned in accordance with the rules laid down in Commission Regulation (EEC) No 2467/79; they must have been approved by the Member State concerned.

Payments are made through agencies appointed by the Member State concerned. Advances of up to 80% of the Community contribution may be granted. The payment arrangements are set out in Commission Regulation (EEC) No 2650/80.

Common measure for forestry in certain Mediterranean zones of the Community (Council Regulation (EEC) No 269/79 as amended by Council Regulation (EEC) No 2119/83)

Eligibility and selection criteria

The Fund may grant aid to finance special programmes forming part of an outline programme which relate to forestry measures and consist of one or more physical investment projects to be implemented on public, semi-public or private land. Aid is provided for afforestation, improvement of deteriorated forest, associated work such as terracing and other minor soil stabilization operations, fire protection, construction of forest roads and specific studies and trials necessary for the implementation of the outline programme. The eligible regions are:

(i) in Italy:
the Mezzogiorno, Lazio, Tuscany, Liguria, Umbria, Marche, Emilia-Romagna and the provinces of Cuneo and Alessandria in Piedmont and Pavia in Lombardy;

(ii) in France:
the regions of Languedoc-Roussilon, Provence-Côte d'Azur and Corsica and the departments of Ardèche and Drôme.

Information to be included in the outline programme is specified in Articles 2 to 5 of Regulation (EEC) No 269/79 and information to be included in the special programme in Articles 6 and 7 of that Regulation.

Financial provisions

The Fund's participation rate is 50% of the cost of executing the eligible project. The contribution of the Member State concerned must be at least 40% and that of the owner of the land at least 5% (except in certain cases).

Procedures

The outline programme must be forwarded to the Commission by the Member State concerned. The agency responsible for implementing the special programme must submit its application for aid through the Member State concerned in accordance with Commission Regulation (EEC) No 2468/78. The special programme must have been approved by the Member State concerned.

Payments are made through agencies appointed by the Member State concerned. Advances of up to 80% of the Community contribution to the cost of one year's work on forestry operations may be granted. Payment arrangements are laid down in Commission Regulation (EEC) No 2416/80.

Collective projects for the restructuring of vineyards (Council Regulation (EEC) No 458/80 as amended by Council Regulations (EEC) No 2991/81 and No 1598/83)

Eligibility and selection criteria

The EAGGF Guidance Section may grant aid in the form of a refund of part of the expenditure incurred by Member States for collective restructuring projects.

The eligible areas are vineyards producing table wines and those suitable for production of quality wines psr, with the exception of:

(i) areas classified in Category 3 as defined in Articles 29 and 29a of Council Regulation (EEC) No 337/79 on the common organization of the market in wine;

(ii) vineyards in the Languedoc-Roussillon region and in the departments of Ardèche, Bouches-du-Rhône, Var and Vaucluse for the duration of the action provided for in Council Directive 78/627/EEC on the programme to accelerate the restructuring and conversion of vineyards in certain Mediterranean regions in France;

(iii) vineyards in the Charentes region intended for the production of wine suitable for the production of certain spirits with registered designations of origin (with the exception of areas of vineyard replanted to produce table wines or quality wines psr up to a limit of 1 000 hectares).

Eligible projects are projects for the replanting of vineyards undertaken by growers under a binding agreement concluded between them.

Other eligibility conditions, relate of minimum restructured areas (e. g. in the case of table wines, an area of not less than 100 hectares, made up of unbroken wine-growing areas which are in principle not less than 2 hectares each).

Projects must contribute to a lasting improvement in working conditions and labour income, guarantee an improvement in the quality of the wines produced and offer an adequate guarantee as to their economic effectiveness.

Financial provisions

Aid in respect of the restructuring of vineyards is granted in the form of a premium per hectare of vineyard replanted or newly planted. The Member State concerned fixes the amount of the premium at between 2 418 and 3 022 ECU per hectare on the basis of the structural situation and the cost of the work.

The maximum premium may be exceeded under special circumstances, but the additional cost must be met by the Member States. In the case of new planting, the eligible amount may not exceed 2 418 ECU per hectare.

The EAGGF Guidance Section refunds 30% of the eligible expenditure to the Member States up to a limit of 240 600 hectares of replanted or newly planted vineyard (including a maximum of 45 600 hectares of vineyard which produced quality wines psr for the wine-growing year preceding the year of grubbing-up).

Procedures

Projects must be submitted by the Member State concerned. The must have been approved by the Member State in whose territory they are to be implemented.

The information to be provided on projects and the form in which they are to be presented are laid down in Commission Regulation (EEC) No 1679/81 (as amended by Commission Regulation (EEC) No 3397/82).

Applications for refunds relate to expenditure incurred by Member States in the course of one calendar year and are submitted to the Commission before 1 July of the following year. Advances may be granted by the Fund, arrangements for which are laid down in Commission Decision 81/525/EEC.

Improving public amenities in certain less-favoured agricultural areas of the Federal Republic of Germany (Council Regulation (EEC) No 1938/81)

Eligibility and selection criteria

The Fund may grant assistance to physical investment projects in the public, semi-public or private sectors which are included in an outline programme drawn up by the Federal Republic of Germany and covering:

(i) water engineering measures for agricultural purposes, including the building of reservoirs, the regulation of water courses and flood control;

(ii) the construction and improvement of farm and local roads which are mainly used for agriculture and forestry.

The projects must be located in certain less-favoured agricultural areas of the Federal Republic of Germany within the meaning of Directives 75/268/EEC and 75/270/EEC. These areas are defined in Article 1 of Regulation (EEC) No 1938/81.

Projects for which Community aid is provided under other EAGGF Guidance Section measures or under the European Development Fund are not eligible. The common measure should normally last until June 1986.

Financial provisions

The subsidy granted by the Fund is 30%; the financial contribution of the Federal Republic of Germany must be at least 20% and that of the beneficiary at least 10%.

Procedures

Fund aid may be granted to the natural or legal persons, or groups thereof, who are ultimately responsible for the cost of carrying out the project.

The aid from the Fund is paid through agencies designated for the Member State concerned.

Integrated development programme for the less-favoured areas of Belgium (Council Regulation (EEC) No 1941/81)

Eligibility and selection criteria

The EAGGF Guidance Section can finance certain projects which form part of an integrated development programme for less-favoured agricultural areas within the meaning of Directive 75/269/EEC. This programme, which is transmitted to the Commission by the Kingdom of Belgium, covers not only measures to improve agriculture and operations to improve the marketing and processing of agricultural products, but also measures to improve infrastructure, to develop tourism, the crafts sector and industry and other complementary activities essential to the improvement of the general socio-economic situation of the region.

Projects eligible for aid from the EAGGF Guidance Section are physical investment projects in the public, semi-public or private sectors and any specific operation in connection with the following measures:

(i) the indentification and analysis of problems at farm level in the context of the programme and the implementation of solutions;

(ii) the development of experimental centres for new lines of production agricultural techniques and farm management;

(iii) the improvement of agricultural infrastructure.

Projects eligible for Community aid under other EAGGF Guidance Section measures or receiving aid under the European Regional Development Fund are not eligible.

The common measure lasts for five years as from the date of notification of the Commission's opinion on the integrated development programme transmitted by the Belgian authorities.

Financial provisions

Aid from the Fund consists of capital grants not exceeding 35% of the actual cost of the project. In the case of the indentification and analysis of problems at farm level, the actual cost covers only operating costs and not administrative expenses or the cost of establishing new farms. The Kingdom of Belgium must also help to finance each project.

Procedures

Aid from the Fund is granted to the natural or legal persons or groups thereof who are ultimately responsible for the cost of carrying out the project.

Applications for aid must be submitted through the Kingdom of Belgium.

Payments from the Fund are made by agencies appointed for that purpose by the Kingdom of Belgium.

Restructuring, modernization and development of the fishing industry and development of aquaculture (Council Regulation (EEC) No 2908/83)

The measure is described in Chapter II of this part.

Acceleration of collective irrigation operations in Greece (Council Regulation (EEC) No 2968/83 as amended by Council Regulation (EEC) No 1302/84)

The duration of the measure is normally limited to two years (1984-85).

Eligibility and selection criteria

Community aid is granted to one or more special irrigation programmes. Eligible irrigation programmes involve collective irrigation operations using existing resources, including the necessary associated drainage work.

They must promote the development of types of crop production that meet market requirements and an indication must be given of the measures to be taken:

(i) to ensure that irrigation of vines for winemaking is excluded from the collective irrigation operations envisaged;

(ii) to encourage farm conversion to the growing of fodder crops (maize, barley, lucerne, clover, field beans, sorghum, soya, fodder beet, etc.) and to livestock farming.

Financial provisions

Fund aid consist of capital grants paid in one or more instalments.

Aid from the Fund covers 50% of the cost of public water supply works not yet started, within the maximum limit of the cost per hectare irrigated of 5 000 ECU.

The Fund may grant advances on the basis of the annual segments of the public works to be carried out under a special programme. Advances may not exceed 80% of the Comunity contribution to the estimated cost of an annual segment of the public works.

Procedures

Applications for aid from the Fund for special programmes must be submitted through the Hellenic Government.

The Commission decides on aid from the Fund after consulting the Fund Comittee (made up of representatives of the Member States) on the financial aspects. The Hellenic Government and the public authority responsible for implementing the special programme are notified of the Commission's decision.

B. Indirect measures

A number of indirect measures are carried out on the Community's intitiative and with its financial help (ranging from 25% to 65%) but they are executed by the Member States. These measures are listed in Table I.

Interested public or private bodies should contact the Ministry of Agriculture in their own Member State for details of the procedures for submitting applications.

TABLE I

EAGGF Guidance Section: Direct and indirect measures

DIRECT MEASURES*

Legal basis	OJ L series	Date	Description
1. Reg. No 355/77 [1]	51/1	23. 02. 1977	Improving the conditions under which agricultural and fisheries products are processed and marketed
2. Reg. No 1760/78 [2]	204/1	28. 07. 1978	Improving public amenities in certain rural areas
3. Reg. No 269/79 [3]	38/1	14. 02. 1979	Common measure for forestry in certain Mediterranean areas of the Community
4. Reg. No 458/80 [4]	57/27	29. 02. 1980	Collective projects for the restructuring of vineyards
5. Reg. No 1938/81	197/1	20. 07. 1981	Improving public amenities in certain less-favoured areas of the Federal Republic of Germany
6. Reg. No 1941/81	197/13	20. 07. 1981	Integrated development programme for less-favoured areas of Belgium
7. Reg. No 2969/83 [5]	293/5	25. 10. 1983	Acceleration of collective irrigation operations in Greece

INDIRECT MEASURES **

Legal basis	OJ L series	Date	Description
a) Socio-structural measures			
8. Dir. 72/159 [6]	96/1	23. 04. 1972	Modernization of farms
9. Dir. 72/160 [6]	96/9	23. 04. 1972	Cessation of farming and the reallocation of utilized agricultural area for the purposes of structural improvement
10. Dir. 72/161 [6]	96/15	23. 04. 1972	Socio-economic guidance for and the acquisition of occupational skills by persons engaged in agriculture
11. Dir. 75/268 [6]	128/1	19. 05. 1975	Mountain and hill farming in certain less-favoured areas
b) Indirect measures in favour of less-favoured regions			
12. Dir. 78/627	206/1	29. 07. 1978	Accelerated restructuring and conversion of vineyards in certain Mediterranean regions
13. Dir. 78/628 and Reg. No 2195/81	206/5 214/5	29. 07. 1978 01. 08. 1981	Accelerated drainage in the less-favoured areas of the West of Ireland
14. Dir. 79/173	38/15	14. 02. 1979	Acceleration and guidance of collective irrigation operations in Corsica
15. Dir. 79/174	38/18	14. 02. 1979	Flood protection in the Hérault valley

Legal basis	OJ L series	Date	Description
16. Dir. 79/197	43/23	20. 09. 1979	Programme to promote drainage in catchment areas common to Ireland and Northern Ireland
17. Dir. 79/359	85/34	05. 09. 1979	Programme to speed up the conversion of certain areas under vines in the Charentes region
18. Reg. No 270/79	38/6	14. 02. 1979	Development of agricultural advisory services in Italy
19. Reg. No 1820/80 [7]	180/1	14. 07. 1980	Stimulation of agricultural development in the less-favoured areas of the West of Ireland
20. Reg. No 1821/180	180/9	14. 07. 1980	Development of sheep farming in Greenland
21. Reg. No 1054/81	111/1	23. 04. 1981	Common measure for the development of beef cattle production in Ireland and Northern Ireland
22. Reg. No 1939/81	197/6	20. 07. 1981	Integrated development programme for the Western Isles of Scotland
23. Reg. No 1940/81	197/9	20. 07. 1981	Integrated development programme for the department of Lozère (France)
24. Reg. No 1942/81	197/7	20. 07. 1981	Stimulation of agricultural development in Northern Ireland
25. Reg. No 1944/81	197/27	20. 07. 1981	Adaptation and modernization of the structure of production of beef and veal, sheepmeat and goatmeat in Italy
26. Dir. 81/527	197/38	20. 07. 1981	Development of agriculture in the French overseas departments
27. Reg. No 1975/82	214/1	22. 07. 1982	Acceleration of agricultural development in certain regions of Greece
28. Reg. No 2966/83	293/1	25. 10. 1983	Development of agricultural advisory services in Greece
c) Measures concerning the common organization of the markets			
29. Reg. No 2511/69	318/1	18. 12. 1969	Improving production and marketing of Community citrus fruits
30. Reg. No 1696/71	175/1	04. 08. 1971	Common organization of the market in hops
31. Reg. No 1035/72	118/1	20. 05. 1972	Common organization of the market in fruit and vegetables
32. Reg. No 1360/78	166/1	23. 06. 1978	Producer groups and associations thereof
33. Reg. No 456/80	57/6	29. 02. 1980	Temporary and permanent abandonment premiums in respect of certain areas under vines
34. Reg. No 457/80	57/23	29. 02. 1980	Premiums for the cessation of wine growing in France and Italy

Legal basis	OJ L series	Date	Description
35. Reg. No 1055/81	111/4	23. 04. 1981	Temporary financial aid to Ireland for pre-movement tuberculin testing and brucellosis blood sampling of cattle
36. Reg. No 389/82	51/1	23. 02. 1982	Producer groups and associations thereof in the cotton sector
d) Measures in the veterinary field			
37. Dir. 77/391	145/44	13. 06. 1977	Eradication of brucellosis, tuberculosis and leucosis in cattle
38. Dec. 80/1097	325/8	01. 12. 1980	Eradication of African swine fever

* Regulation (EEC) No 2908/83 also falls within the EAGGF Guidance Section (direct measures); it is described in Chapter II of this part.

** Regulation (EEC) No 1772/82 also falls within the EAGGF Guidance Section (indirect measures); it is mentioned in Chapter II of this part.

[1] Amended by Regulation (EEC) No 1932/84 (OJ L 180/1 of 7. 7. 1984).

[2] Amended by Regulation (EEC) No 2003/84 (OJ L 198/1 of 21. 7. 1981)

[3] Amended by Regulation (EEC) No 2119/83 (OJ L 205/4 of 29. 7. 1983).

[4] Amended by Regulation (EEC) No 2991/81 (OJ L 299/21 of 20. 10 1981) and by Regulation (EEC) No 1598/83 (OJ L 163/53 of 22. 6. 1983).

[5] Amended by Regulation (EEC) No 1302/84 (OJ L 125/6 of 12. 5. 1984).

[6] Proposals amending and supplementing these directives have been presented to the Council and are currently being examined.

[7] Amended by Regulation (EEC) No 1932/84 (OJ L 180/1 of 7. 7. 1984).

Chapter II: Measures to improve fishery structures

Aim

The measures described in this chapter are structural measures implemented under the common fisheries policy: either to adjust and redirect capacity or to restructure and develop the industry. Each measure has its own clearly defined objective (see Table II for the list of measures).

Main features

Some of the measures for improving fishery structures are financed by the EAGGF Guidance Section (common measures); the others are financed from Community budget resources allocated to the common fisheries policy (measures to adjust and redirect capacity).

Like those of the EAGGF Guidance Section, the measures described here subdivide into direct and indirect measures. Direct measures relate to Community assistance for private or public investment projects; indirect measures relate to reimbursement by the Fund of expenditure incurred by the Member State for certain measures.

A. Direct measures

Direct measure for restructuring, modernizing and developing the fishing industry and for developing aquaculture (Council Regulation (EEC) No 2908/83)

Eligibility and selection criteria

Projects eligible under this regulation are public, semi-public or private capital investment projects relating entirely or partly to:

(a) the purchase or construction of new fishing vessels, and the modernization or conversion of fishing vessels already in use;

(b) the construction, equipment or modernization of installations for rearing fish, crustaceans and molluscs;

(c) the construction, within an area of three miles from the base lines, of artificial structures to facilitate re-stocking of Mediterranean coastal areas.

Projects must be consistent with the guidelines laid down by the multiannual guidance (or their descriptive summaries) drawn up by the Member States, offer a satisfactory guarantee of yielding a profit and contribute to the lasting economic effect of structural improvement aimed at by the programmes.

The fishing vessels must be between 9 and 33 metres in length. The modernization or conversion work must be substantial and must amount to at least 20 000 ECU per project; this limit is reduced to 10 000 ECU for fishing vessels which are between 9 and 12 metres in length.

The following projects are given priority for Fund aid:

(i) in respect of new fishing vessels, the commissioning of vessels intended to replace vessels more than 12 years old, vessels lost as a result of accident or wreck or vessels based in coastal areas where fishing is traditionally an important economic activity;

(ii) in respect of the modernization of fishing vessels, projects designed to encourage fuel saving, projects which are coordinated in their economic and technical aspects and projects aimed at improving the processing of catches;

(iii) in respect of aquaculture, the launching of pilot projects designed to guide and develop production and to facilitate retraining of fishermen.

Other criteria used in the selection of projects include:

(i) the diversification of economic activity,

(ii) the living and working conditions on board,

(iii) the beneficiary's membership of a producers' organization,

(iv) the requirement for environmental protection,

(v) the interests of consumers.

Special conditions are imposed on recipients of Fund aid in the case of the construction or modernization of fishing vessels; such vessels may not be sold outside the Community, may not normally carry out their activities from a port other than a port situated within the Community and may be withdrawn from fishing, except in cases of *force majeure,* for a period of:

(i) at least 10 years from the date of commissioning of the new vessel;

(ii) at least 5 years from the date on which modernization or conversion work is completed.

Projects which receive Community aid under other common measures of the EAGGF Guidance Section or from the European Regional Development Fund are not eligible.

Financial provisions

Aid from the Fund consists of capital subsidies not exceeding 25% of the cost of the investment; the Member State's contribution must be at least 5% and that of the beneficiary at least 50%.

However, these rates may be more favourable in two cases:

(i) in Greenland (until the end of 1984), Greece, Ireland, Northern Ireland, the Mezzogiorno and the French overseas departments, the Fund aid may amount to 50% of the cost and the beneficiary's contribution must be at least 25%;

(ii) for projects relating to the construction of articificial structures to facilitate re-stocking of Mediterranean coastal areas, the Fund aid may amount to 50% and the beneficiary's contribution must be at least 5%.

Procedures

Fund aid may be granted to the natural or legal persons or groups thereof who are ultimately responsible for the cost of carrying out the project. Applications must be submitted through the Member State concerned after its approval has been obtained. Aid decisions are taken twice yearly: not later than 30 April for applications submitted by 31 October of previous year, and not later than 31 October for applications submitted by 31 March.

The particulars to be given in applications, the form in which they are to be submitted and the arrangements for payment are laid down in Commission Regulation (EEC) No 378/84.

B. Indirect measures

Indirect measures are carried out at the initiative and with the financial assistance (generally 50%) of the Community but are implemented by the Member States.

These measures currently cover:

(i) the encouragement of exploratory fishing and cooperation through joint ventures in the fishing sector;

(ii) the adjustment of capacity in the fishing sector;

(iii) action to encourage the setting up of producer organizations.

Enquiries concerning the procedures for submitting applications may be addressed to the ministry responsible for fisheries in the Member State concerned.

TABLE II

Measures to improve fishery structures

DIRECT MEASURES

Legal basis	OJ L series	Date	Description
1. Reg. 2908/83 (EAGGF Guidance Section)	290	22. 10. 1983	Restructuring, modernizing and developing the fishing industry and developing aquaculture

INDIRECT MEASURES

Legal basis	OJ L series	Date	Description
a) Connected with the adjustment and redirection of capacity			
2. Reg. 2909/83	290	22. 10. 1983	Measures to encourage exploratory fishing and cooperation through joint ventures in the fishing sector
3. Dir. 83/515	290	23. 10. 1983	Measures to adjust capacity in the fisheries sector
b) Measure concerning the common organization of the market			
4. Reg. 3796/81 and Reg. 1772/82 (EAGGF Guidance Section)	379 197	31. 12. 1981 6. 7. 1982	Common organization of the market in fishery products-producer groups

Chapter III — European Social Fund (ESF)

Aim

The aim of the Social Fund is set out in Article 123 of the EEC Treaty: the Fund has 'the task of rendering the employment of workers easier and of increasing their geographical and occupational mobility within the Community'.

TABLE III

European Social Fund: methods of assistance, trypes of operation and categories of persons concerned

A – Methods of assistance within the meaning of Article 3 of Decision 83/516/EEC [1]

Legal basis		Description
1. Dec. 83/516, Art. 3(1)		Operations carried out within the framework of Member States' labour-market policies
2. Dec. 83/516, Art. 3(2)		Specific operations (no more than 5% of appropriations available) (a) innovatory projects (b) examining the effectiveness of projects financed by the Fund and exchange of experience

B – Types of operations within the meaning of Article 1 of Decision 83/516/EEC

Legal basis		Description
3. Dec. 83/516, Art. 1(2)	a)	Vocational training and guidance
	b)	Recruitment and wage subsidies
	c)	Resettlement and socio-vocational integration in connection with geographical mobility
	d)	Services and technical advice concerned with job creation

C – Categories of persons concerned within the meaning of Article 4 of Council Decision 83/516/EEC

Legal basis		Description
4. Art. 4(1)		Young people under the age of 25 (at least 75% of available funds)
5. Art. 4(2)		Persons over the age of 25:
	a)	– people unemployed, threatened with unemployment or under-employed
	b)	– women wishing to return to work
	c)	– handicapped people
	d)	– migrant workers
	e)	– people employed particularly in small or medium-sized firms who need retraining with a view to the introduction of new technology or the improvement of management techniques.
6. Art. 4(3)		People to be engaged as instructors, vocational-guidance or placement experts or development agents.

[1] OJ L 289/38, 22. 10. 1983.

D – Expenditure eligible under implementing Regulation (EEC) No 2950/83

Legal basis		Description
7. Reg. 2950/83, Art. 1	(a)[1]	Incomes of persons undergoing vocational training
	(b)	Costs of: (i) preparation, operation and administration of vocational training measures, including depreciation and vocational guidance (ii) board and lodging, and travelling expenses for the recipients of vocational training (iii) adaptation of workplaces for handicapped persons
	(c)	granting of aid for recruitment and employment of young people under 25 and of the long-term unemployed
	(d)	Transfer and integration of migrant workers and their families
	(e)[1]	Preparatory or evaluation operations or studies

[1] OJ L 289/1, 22. 10. 1983.

Main features of the Social Fund

Council Decision 83/516/EEC on the tasks of the European Social Fund provides for the Fund to assist:

(i) operations carried out within the framework of Member States' labour-market policies. These operations include in particular those intended to improve employment opportunities for young people below the age of 25. It should be noted that less than 75% of all the Fund's available appropriations in any one year must be allocated to projects to help young people;

(ii) specific operations carried out with a view to encouraging the implementation of innovatory projects or to examining the effectiveness of projects for which Fund assistance is granted and facilitating an exchange of experience. The appropriations intended for these specific projects must not be more in any one year than 5% of all the available appropriations.

A further basic feature of the Social Fund is the geographical concentration of its assistance:

(iii) 40% of the total appropriations available for operations carried out within the framework of Member States' labour-market policies go to the following priority countries or regions: Greenland (up to the end of 1984), Greece, the French overseas departments, Ireland, Northern Ireland and the Mezzogiorno.

(iv) The remaining appropriations are channelled to operations to expand employment in areas of high and long-term unemployment and/or industrial and sectoral restructuring.

Eligibility and selection criteria

The eligibility criteria cover types of operations, categories of persons and categories of expenditure.

The Fund may participate in financing operations carried out by private or public operators concerning:

(i) vocational training and guidance;

(ii) recruitment and wage subsidies;

(iii) resettlement and socio-vocational integration in connection with geographical mobility;

(iv) services and technical advice concerned with job creation.

These operations must concern the following categories of persons:

(1) young people under the age of 25, in particular those whose chances of employment are especially poor (because of lack of vocational training or inadequate training) and those who are long-term unemployed;

(2) the following persons over the age of 25:
   (a) people who are unemployed, threatened with unemployment or under-employed, and in particular the long-term unemployed;
   (b) women wishing to return to work;
   (c) handicapped people who are capable of working in the open labour market;
   (d) migrant workers who move or have moved within the Community or become residents in the Community to take up work, together with the members of their families;
   (e) people who are employed particularly in small or medium-sized undertakings and who require retraining with a view to the introduction of new technology or the improvement of management techniques in those undertakings.

(3) people to be engaged as instructors, vocational-guidance or placement experts or development agents.

Under Council Regulation (EEC) No 2950/83, the Fund may grant assistance for expenditure intended to cover:

(a) incomes of persons undergoing vocational training;

(b) the cost of vocational training (preparation, operation and administration; training teaching staff; depreciation costs; vocational guidance, board and lodging and travelling expenses of recipients) and the cost of adapting workplaces for the vocational integration of the handicapped;

(c) the granting of employment aids (aid for recruitment or employment) in projects for the creation of additional jobs for job-seekers under 25 and for the long-term unemployed. Such aid may be granted only for a period not exceeding 12 months per person;

(d) benefits designed to facilitate the transfer and integration of migrant workers and their families;

(e) preparatory or evaluation operations or studies.

The appropriations for the different operations of the Social Fund are entered under separate budget items (young people under 25 and people over 25, with a distinction being made between less-favoured regions and other regions with high unemployment; specific operations). The total volume of applications for assistance frequently far exceeds the available budget appropriations, with the result that a selection of operations has to be made.

In order to provide an objective basis for carrying out this selection, the Commission adopts, before 1 May of each year and for the following three financial years, the Fund-management guidelines for determining those operations which reflect Community priorities. These guidelines are published in the *Official Journal of the European Communities*. Those for the period 1985-87 were published in Official Journal C 126/3 of 12. 5. 1984.

The guidelines serve to determine the types of operation regarded by the Commission as having priority and the list of other areas of high and long-term unemployment and/or industrial and sectoral restructuring situated outside less-favoured countries or regions which are allocated 40% of the available commitment appropriations.

The Commission approves the eligible applications for assistance by budget item, beginning with the priority applications.

If the volume of eligible applications exceeds the available appropriations, a reduction is applied, either on an across-the board basis (for applications relating to less-favoured regions) or on a weighted basis for the other regions, in which case account is taken of the relative severity of imbalances in the labour market (unemployment rates and the Member States' economic capacity for correcting them (per capita GDP).

Financial provisions

Fund assistance is granted at the rate of 50% of eligible expenditure, but must not exceed the financial contribution of the public authorities of the Member State concerned. Thus, in the case of private sector projects (where at least 10% of the eligible expenditure is borne by profit-making bodies), the amount of Fund assistance is equal to whatever aid is provided by the public authorities, provided that the public authorities guarantee successful completion of the operations.

Fund assistance is granted on a flat-rate basis in the case of employment aids (recruitment and employment) for young job-seekers below the age of 25 and for the long-term unemployed. The aid granted amounts to 15% of the gross average wage of industrial workers in the Member State concerned. Before 1 August of each year, the Commission publishes the amounts of assistance to be granted during the following year, per person and per unit of time.

Fund assistance is increased by 10% for operations to expand employment in regions where there is an especially serious and prolonged imbalance in employment, namely Greenland (up to the end of 1984), Greece, the French overseas departments, Ireland, Northern Ireland and the Mezzogiorno.

In the case of specific operations to examine the effectiveness of projects for which Fund assistance has been granted and which are carried out on the initiative of the Commission, assistance covers the total eligible expenditure. Member States are not required to guarantee the successful completion of such operations.

Procedures

Fund assistance may be given for operations carried out both by bodies governed by public law and bodies governed by private law, provided that the public authorities guarantee the successful completion of the operations. Applications for Fund assistance in respect of operations carried out within the framework of Member States' labour-market policies may only be submitted through the Member State concerned. Applications relating to expenditure to be incurred in the following year or, in the case of specific operations, during the following years must be submitted by the Member States by 21 October of each year. An exception is made in the case of urgent applications, which must be submitted by the Member States at least one month before the operation begins.

The Commission decides on applications for assistance before 31 March of the relevant financial year. This date may be later if the Community's general budget is itself adopted after 1 March of the relevant financial year.

The approval of an application for assistance in respect of operations carried out within the framework of Member States' labour-market policies is followed by the payment of an advance of 50% of the assistance approved on the date on which the operations are sheduled to begin. Where this date precedes the date of the decision of approval, payment is made immediately after that decision.

The approval of an application submitted in respect of specific operations is followed by the payment of a first advance equal to 30% of the assistance granted. A second advance of 30% may be paid when the Member State concerned certifies that half the operation has been completed in accordance with the conditions set out in the decision of approval.

Final payment claims must contain a detailed report on the content, results and financial aspects of the operation.

All the administrative rules governing the submission of applications for assistance and payment claims are set out in Commission Decision 83/673/EEC[1]. Specimen forms to be used by the Member States when submitting applications for assistance and payment claims are annexed to this decision.

(1) OJ L 377 of 31. 12. 1983

Chapter IV: European Regional Development Fund (ERDF)

Aim

The aim of the European Regional Development Fund is to help correct the principal regional imbalances within the Community by contributing to the development and structural adjustment of regions with a development lag and to the conversion of declining industrial regions.

TABLE IV

Operations of the Regional Fund
(Council Regulation (EEC) No 1787/84 - OJ L 169 of 28. 6. 1984)

A – Types of operation

Legal basis	Description
1. Reg. No 1787/84, Article 5	Community programmes National programmes of Community interest Projects Studies

B – Operations financed

Legal basis	Description
2. Reg. No 1787/84 Article 7 and 10	*Community programmes and national programmes of Community interest:* (i) aid schemes for industry, the craft sector and services (ii) infrastructure investment (iii) operations to exploit potential for internally generated development
3. Article 15	*Measures to exploit potential for internally generated development:* 1. Industry, the craft sector and tourism: (i) surveys of opportunities for internally generated development (ii) applied research organizations working to further internally generated development (iii) technology transfers (iv) sectoral studies (v) access to management and organization advisory services (vi) establishment of common services (vii) promotion and coordinated management of accommodation (tourism) (viii) access to the capital market 2. Contributions to public expenditure on the planning, preparation and implementation of operations submitted to the Regional Fund
4. Article 17	*Investment projects:* (i) in industry, the craft and services sectors (ii) infrastructure projects
5. Article 24	*Studies:* (i) closely related to Fund operations (ii) on the effective use of Fund resources

Main features of the Regional Fund

The operation of the Regional Fund is set out in Council Regulation (EEC) No 1787/84. As from 1985, all of the Regional Fund's resources are allocated on the basis of ranges of which the lower and upper limits are fixed for each Member State as follows:

Belgium	0.90 to 1.20%	Ireland	5.64 to 6.83%
Denmark	0.51 to 0.67%	Italy	31.94 to 42.59%
Germany	3.76 to 4.81%	Luxembourg	0.06 to 0.08%
Greece	12.35 to 15.74%	Netherlands	1.00 to 1.34%
France	11.05 to 14.74%	United Kingdom	21.42 to 28.56%

These upper and lower limits apply for periods of three years. The lower limit of the range constitutes the minimum amount of ERDF resources each Member State is guaranteed if it submits an adequate volume of eligible grant applications to the Commission: the allocation of Regional Fund resources between the lower and upper limits depends on the compliance by each Member State with the priorities and criteria laid down in the Regulation.

The Fund helps to finance Community programmes, national programmes of Community interest, projects and studies. The proportion of ERDF aid allocated to programme financing is to be increased gradually to reach, if possible, at least 20% of its approriations by the end of 1987.

Finally, assistance from the Regional Fund may, in accordance with a prior decision by the Member State communicated at the same time as the grant application, either supplement national aid granted to the investment by the public authorities or remain in the hands of those authorities as a partial reimbursement of such aid.

Eligibility and selection criteria

(1) Participation in financing Community programmes

A Community programme is defined as a series of consistent multiannual measures directly serving Community objectives and the implementation of Community policies. Such programmes are undertaken on the initiative of the Commission and are intended to help solve serious problems affecting the socio-economic situation in one or more regions.

As a rule they concern the territory of more than one Member State, with their agreement.

The purpose of Community programmes is to promote, the establishment of new economic activities, the creation of alternative employment in regions or areas in a difficult situation; they may not, however, have as their object the internal reorganization of declining sectors.

The types of operations eligible for Community programmes primarily include:

(i) aid schemes for industry, the craft sector or services;

(ii) infrastructure investment (except for certain categories excluded by the regulation);

(iii) operations to exploit the potential for internally generated development.

The nature and practical details of the operations are determined case by case. The same applies to the targets, the areas and regions eligible, the financing plan, the categories of beneficiaries, the financing arrangements, the provisions relating to publicity and any related measures necessary for the implementation of the programmes.

In the management of Regional Fund resources, priority is given to Community programmes.

(2) Participation in financing national programmes of Community interest

National programmes of Community interest are drawn up at national level and consist of a set of consistent multiannual measures corresponding to national objectives and serving Community objectives and policies.

Such measures may concern, jointly or separately:

(i) infrastructure investment (except for certain categories excluded by the regulation);

(ii) aid schemes for industry, the craft sector and services

(iii) operations to exploit the potential for internally generated development.

The regions and areas which the Regional Fund may assist through national programmes of Community interest ar limited to the assisted areas designated by Member States for the purposes of their regional aid schemes.

The Commission assesses national programmes of Community interest on the basis of their consistency with regional development programmes and their contribution to the Community's objectives and priorities, and primarily those of regional policy.

(3) Participation in the financing of measures to exploit the potential for internally generated development of regions (**co-financing within the framework programmes or coordinated series of projects**)

In order to harness, a region's potential for internally generated development, the Regional Fund may contribute to the financing of coordinated series of measures for assisting undertakings, primarily small businesses, undertakings in industry and the craft and tourism sectors; the measures must:

(i) provide those undertakings with facilities enabling them to expand their activities and to obtain access to new technology,

(ii) facilitate their access to the capital market.

The main measures eligible for financing under this heading include:

(i) surveys on the opportunities for internally generated regional development eligible for Regional Fund aid;

(ii) the setting up and operation of applied research organizations whose object is to further internally generated regional development;

(iii) in the case of small and medium-sized undertakings: technology transfers, sectoral studies, access to management and organization advisory services, the establishment of common services, the promotion and coordinated management of tourist accommodation, access to the capital market for small businesses;

(iv) besides the measures to assist undertakings, the Regional Fund may also make a contribution to public expenditure on the planning, technical preparation and implementation of operations which are the subject of applications for Regional Fund aid.

Aid for measures to exploit potential for internally generated development may not last longer than three years for the same recipient and the same project. Nor may the aggregate of Fund aid and national aid to such undertakings exceed 80% of the expenditure incurred by them.

(4) Participation in the financing of investment projects

The Regional Fund may contribute to the financing of investment projects costing more than 50 000 ECU each in industry, in the crafts or services sector or in infrastructure. To benefit from Fund assistance, investment projects must fall within the framework of regional development programmes prepared in accordance with a common outline and transmitted to the Commission by the Member States. Regions and areas in which projects may be assisted by the ERDF must be assisted areas designated by Member States for the purposes of their regional aid schemes.

Infrastructure investment projects which may be assisted by the Fund are those:

(i) which contribute to the development of the region or area in which they are located. Certain categories of infrastructure are excluded by the Fund Regulation (e. g. establishments of general education and hospitals (except in regions with a severe shortage of such facilities), residential care facilities, administrative buildings, housing, etc.), or

(ii) for which the cost is borne wholly or partly by public authorities or by any other organization responsible, in the same way as a public authority, for carrying out infrastructure projects.

Exceptionally, the Fund may grant aid to infrastructure investment projects not located in an eligible region or area but situated in an area adjacent to such a region or area and which are an essential complement to its infrastructure (the amount of Fund resources allocated to such investment projects may not exceed 4% of its total resources).

Investment projects in industry or the craft or services sector, to be eligible for assistance, must relate to economically sound activities which are intended to help create or maintain permanent jobs.

Where the aim is to preserve jobs, the investments must fall within a conversion or restructuring plan ensuring that the establishment concerned is competitive.

Activities in the service sector qualifying for assistance are those concerning tourism or those having a choice of location; they must have an impact on the development of the region and on the level of employment.

The types of official aid to be taken into consideration in determining Regional Fund assistance are grants or subsidies, interest-rate subsidies or their equivalent where loans at reduced rates of interest are concerned, and any other form of quantifiable investment aid. Such aid may be linked to the amount of investment or to the number of jobs created.

(5) Co-financing or financing of studies

The Regional Fund may:

(i) contribute, at the request of or in agreement with the Member States concerned, to the financing of studies which are closely related to its operations;

(ii) defray all or part of the cost of studies covering problems of special significance for the effective use of the Fund's resources.

As a final comment on the selection criteria, it should be noted that investments and measures which form part of an integrated development approach, for example in the form of integrated operations or programmes, may be accorded priority treatment in the management of the Regional Fund's resources.

Financial Provisions

The rates of Regional Fund assistance are generally 50% or 55% of public expenditure. By type of operation, these rates are as follows:

(i) a maximum of 55% of the public expenditure taken into account in Community programmes; the level of participation is determined in the light of the socio-economic situation in the regions and the types of measure planned under the programmes;

(ii) 50% of the total public expenditure taken into account in national programmes of Community interest. This rate may rise to 55% for programmes of particular importance for the regions or areas in which they are located;

(iii) 50% to 55% in the case of measures to exploit a region's potential for internally generated development; the contribution for each study or survey may not exceed 100 000 ECU; the Fund's contribution to the financing of these indigenous development measures may not normally exceed 10% of the minimum appropriations allocated to each Member State in a three-year period;

(iv) 50% of official aid for investment projects in industry and the craft and service sectors;

(v) 50% of the expenditure met by the public authorities in the case of infrastructure investment projects where the investment is less than 15 million ECU; 30% to 50% where the investment is 15 million ECU or more. These rates may rise to 55% for projects of particular importance to the development of the region concerned;

(vi) 50% of the cost of studies related to Fund operations; this rate may rise to 70% of the cost where the studies are of exceptional interest; the Fund may defray the total cost, of studies relating to the effective use of Regional Fund resources

Procedures

Only the competent authorities in the Member States may submit grant applications to the Commission. The decision-making procedures vary according to the type of operation:

(i) Community programmes: on a proposal from the Commission, the Council adopts the outline of each Community programme; this outline covers the specific objectives, the regions or criteria for determining territorial scope, the nature and methods of the operations and the level of Community participation. The programme is then drawn up by the competent authorities of the Member States concerned in consultation with the Commission; it is then adopted by the Commission after the Regional Fund Committee has been consulted;

(ii) national programmes of Community interest: these programmes are undertaken on the initiative of Member States; they are submitted to the Commission by the Member State concerned after having been drawn up by the latter in collaboration with the authorities or bodies concerned. The Commission assesses the programmes and then transmits them to the Member States concerned with its observations. When a programme has been agreed upon by the Commission and the Member State or States concerned it is adopted by the Commission after the Regional Fund Committee has been consulted;

(iii) measures to exploit internally generated development potential the Community co-finances these measures under programmes or coordinated sets of projects. The appropriate procedures (programmes or projects) then apply;

(iv) projects: grant applications are submitted to the Commission by the Member States: either in the form of grouped applications in the case of projects costing less than 15 million ECU or as individual applications in the case of projects costing 15 million ECU or more. The Commission takes the grant decisions, having consulted the Regional Fund Committee beforehand on projects costing 5 million ECU or more and informing that Committee of other projects afterwards.

(v) studies: up to a limit of 0.3% of the Regional Fund's annual endowment, the Commission decides on assistance and informs the Fund Committee; above that limit and up to 0.5% of the annual endowment, assistance is decided on by the Commission after the Fund Committee has been consulted.

Briefly, the main provisions regarding payments made by the Fund are as follows:

(i) for programmes and measures to exploit internally generated development potential, advances may be granted at the request of the Member State for each annual progress made a first advance of not more than 40% at the start of the operations; when half of this first advance has been spent, a second may be made; the two advances together may not exceed 80% of the total committed. The balance of each instalment is paid when the operations have been completed and on submission by the Member States of a statement of the public expenditure incurred;

(ii) a similar system of two advances and payment of the balance may be applied to projects; it then applies not to annual instalments but to the total Fund assistance for each project.

Specific Community measures adopted under the former Regional Fund Regulation

The Former rules governing the Regional Fund, which were based on Regulation (EEC) No 724/75, have been repealed; however, the specific Community regional development measures which came into force before the end of 1984 are still being carried out.

The Community is co-financing specific five-year programmes covering a range of operations designed to meet the specific needs of a number of Community regions.

In 1980 the Council adopted an initial series of specific measures, which were extended and supplemented by new decisions in 1984. The measures currently being implemented are as follows:

(i) Development of certain French and Italian regions (Regulation (EEC) No 214/84 amending Regulation (EEC) No 2615/80) and of certain Greek regions (Regulation (EEC) No 215/84) in the context of Community enlargement: Aquitaine, Languedoc-Roussillon and Midi-Pyrénées in France, the regions of the Mezzogiorno in Italy and the Greek islands with the exception of those not covered by a national regional aid scheme. The special programmes implemented under these measures are designed to reinforce economic structures and create jobs in the recipient regions, particularly through the development of small business and the craft sector, the promotion of innovation and the exploitation of tourist potential.

(ii) Development of new economic activities in certain areas adversely affected by restructuring of:

(a) the steel industry (Regulation (EEC) No 216/84 amending Regulation (EEC) No 2616/80). This measure covers steel areas in Belgium, the Netherlands, the Federal Republic of Germany, Luxembourg, Italy, the United Kingdom and France. Its territorial scope may be extended on the basis of programmes for restructuring the steel industy transmitted by the Member States under Decision 2320/81/ECSC;

(b) the shipbuilding industry (Regulation (EEC) No 217/84 amending Regulation (EEC) No 2617/80). This measure covers areas in the United Kingdom (Strathclyde, Cleveland, Tyne and Wear, Merseyside and Belfast) and the labour-market region of Lübeck-Ostholstein in the Federal Republic of Germany;

(c) the textile and clothing industry (Regulation (EEC) No 219/84). This measure covers areas in Belgium, France, Ireland, Italy, the United Kingdom and the Netherlands.

The purpose of these three measures is to contribute to the development of job-creating activities by improving the physical environment of the areas concerned (an essential pre-condition if such activities are to be created), developing small business and encouraging innovation. The operations must not be concerned with the internal restructuring of declining sectors.

(iii) Improving security of energy supply in certain Community regions by way of improved use of new techniques for hydroelectric power and alternative energy sources (Regulation (EEC) No 218/84 amending Regulation (EEC) No 2618/80). This measure covers the mountainous areas of the Mezzogiorno within the meaning of Council Directive 75/268/EEC and the Greek islands with the exception of Salamis. The measure's aims are: to ensure a better use of hydroelectric resources in those areas and of alternative energy sources; to encourage private users themselves to exploit those energy sources by means of an information campaign and aid for feasibility studies; and to provide additional jobs on the maintenance of the installations.

(iv) Improving the economic and social situation in the border areas of Ireland and Northern Ireland (Regulation (EEC) No 2619/80). This measure covers the counties of Ireland and the council districts of Northern Ireland directly adjoining the border, and its aim to help improve the employment situation by developing economic activities in tourism, communications, the craft industries sector and small business.

Finally, when the Council adopted the second series of specific measures in January 1984, the Commission stated that it had plans for proposing further specific measures: one concerning the areas affected by the Community fisheries policy and the other Ireland and Northern Ireland.

Chapter V — Financial activities of the ECSC (loans and aids, see Table V)

Aim

The European Coal and Steel Community (ECSC) shall progressively bring about conditions which will of themselves ensure the most rational distribution of production at the highest possible level of productivity, while safeguarding continuity of employment and taking care not to provoke fundamental and persistent disturbances in the economies of Member States (Article 2, second paragraph, of the ECSC Treaty).

Main features of ECSC financial operations

The financial operations of the ECSC form a coherent instrument for assistance to the coal and steel industries. They include loans, guarantees and non-repayable grants. The loans fall into three categories: industrial loans under Article 54 ECSC; conversion loans under Article 56; and loans for workers' housing under Article 54.

Grants are made under:

(i) Articles 54 and 56, in the form of interest rebates on industrial loans and conversion loans;

(ii) Article 56 (2) (b) for occupational redeployment of workers and social measures accompanying the restructuring of the coal and steel industries;

(iii) Article 55, for technical, economic and social research;

(iv) Article 46, for the financing of economic and social studies; and

(v) Article 95, for coking coal and coke for the steel industry.

(1) Industrial loans and interest rebates (Article 54)

Eligibility and selection criteria

Under Article 54 of the ECSC Treaty, the following are eligible for assistance:

(a) loans to the coal and steel industries in line with Community policy for those industries.

(b) works and installations which contribute to increasing the production, reducing the production cost or facilitating the marketing of coal and steel products.

(c) loans to enterprises (other than power stations and coking plants), public establishments and local authorities for investment to promote the consumption of Community coal for a minimum period of five years save with the Commission's prior agreement, these loans may not exceed 15 million ECU.

Loans at normal rates are usually granted by the Commission at the rate ruling on the capital market with no extra charge. They thus reflect the rate paid by the ECSC itself on the financial markets on which it has borrowed funds. The loan may not exceed 50% of the agreed project cost.

Some categories of investment can receive loans at a reduced rate of interest (see Table IV). Such assisted loans are granted at the normal interest rate, and the Commission grants an interest rebate which is paid to the beneficiary at the date laid down in the operational budget of the ECSC. The amount of the rebate is three percentage points per year for the first five years of the loan. The Commission determines on a case-by-case basis the portion of the investment (and of the loan) which is eligible for an interest rebate.

Procedures

Applications for industrial loans must be made directly to the Commission by the companies concerned. They must be sent in triplicate to the Commission of the European Communities, Directorate-General for Credit and Investments, Jean Monnet Building, Luxembourg-Kirchberg. This Directorate-General can be contacted for more detailed information on industrial loans.

For investment to promote the consumption of Community coal, loan applications may be sent to a financial intermediary in receipt of an ECSC global loan (see list of financial intermediaries below).

(2) Conversion loans and interest rebates (Article 56)

Eligibility and selection criteria

Investments eligible are those which, by the creation of new and economically sound activities, are capable of reabsorbing into productive employment redundant coal and steel workers. The investment may be in the expansion of an existing production facility, or the creation of a new one. On 16 July 1983 the Commission published detailed rules for conversion loans (OJ C 191).

Financial provisions

Loans may not exceed 50% of the estimated project cost. They are granted at the normal rate of interest; an interest subsidy of three percentage points over five years may be granted in respect of a maximum amount of 20 000 ECU per job to be created which the borrower undertakes to offer in the first place to former ECSC industry workers.

In the case of sub-loans granted through the intermediary of financial institutions the interest subsidy may be increased to five percentage points over five years for a period limited to that of the restructuring of the steel industry.

In ECSC employment areas where loans have not yet created half the jobs lost in the coal and steel industries, the eligibility criteria can be held to be satisfied in respect of a standard proportion of jobs.

In the priority employment areas, the list of which is updated regularly, beneficiaries must notify the new jobs to be created to the competent employment offices and the local ECSC undertakings likely to be shedding workers. In the other ECSC employment areas, beneficiaries must give priority to the recruitment of former ECSC workers.

Outside the ECSC employment areas, the final amount of the interest rebate is calculated on the number of former ECSC workers made redundant and actually re-employed

Procedures

Conversion loans may be granted directly to private undertakings and public bodies in the form of individual loans, or indirectly, in the form of sub-loans, through the intermediary of financial institutions to which the ECSC has granted a global loan. Applications for direct loans must be sent to the Commission of the European Communities through the intermediary of the responsible department of the national government concerned.

Undertakings [1] may apply for a sub-loan of up to 7.5 million ECU from the financial institutions to which a global loan has been granted. The cost of the investment project which is the subject of the application may not exceed 15 million ECU. Priority is given to borrowers employing fewer than 500 people and in whose capital structure large enterprises hold no more than a one-third participation. At the present time, global loan funds are available from the following financial institutions:

BELGIUM

— Société générale de Banque, rue Montagne du Parc 3 — B-1000 Brussels Tel.: (02) 516 21 11
— Banque Bruxelles Lambert, avenue Marnix 24-B-1050 Brussels— Tel.: (02) 517 21 11
— Caisse Nationale de Crédit Professionnel, avenue des Arts 8 — B-1040 Brussels — Tel.: (02) 218 44 20

FEDERAL REPUBLIC OF GERMANY

— Saarländische Investitionskreditbank, Johannisstraße 2, Postfach 8 83 — D-6600 Saarbrücken — Tel.: (0681) 3 60 61
— Industriekreditbank, Karl-Theodor-Straße 6, Postfach 11 18 — D-4000 Düsseldorf 1 — Tel.: (0211) 8 22 11
— Westdeutsche Landesbank Girozentrale, Friedrichstraße 56, Postfach 11 28 — D-4000 Düsseldorf — Tel.: (0211) 82 601
— Deutsche Bank AG, Königsallee 45/47 — D-4000 Düsseldorf — Tel.: (0211) 88 30
— Bayerische Hypotheken- und Wechsel-Bank, Theatinerstraße 11, Postfach 20 05 27 — D-8000 München — Tel.: (089) 2 36 60
— Bayerische Landesbank Girozentrale, Postfach 20 05 25 — D-8000 München 2 — Tel.: (089) 21 71 01
— Bayerische Vereinsbank, Kardinal-Faulhaberstraße 1 und 14 — D-8000 München 2 — Tel.: (089) 2 13 21
— Westfalenbank, Hüstraße 21-25, Postfach 10 27 10 — D-4630 Bochum 1 — Tel.: (0234) 61 61
— Bank für Gemeinwirtschaft, Theaterplatz 2, Postfach 22 44 — D-6000 Frankfurt/Main 1 — Tel.: (069) 25 80
— Dresdner Bank AG Zentrale, Jürgen Ponto-Platz 1, Postfach 11 06 61 — D-6000 Frankfurt/Main 11 — Tel.: (069)26 31
— WGZ-Bank (Westdeutsche Genossenschafts-Zentralbank AG, Sentmaringer Weg 1 — D-4400 Münster 1 — Tel.: (0251) 7 06 00

FRANCE

— Lordex, 109 Boulevard d'Haussonville — F-54041 Nancy Cedex — Tel.: (28) 27 05 22
— Banque populaire de Lorraine, 3 rue François de Curel, Boîte Postale 124 — F-57021 Metz — Tel.: (8) 769 24 12
— Crédit industriel d'Alsace et de Lorraine (CIAL), 4 avenue Robert Schumann, Boîte Postale 48 — F-57021 Metz Cedex — Tel.: (8) 774 91 52
— Banque populaire du Nord, 66 boulevard de la liberté — F-59000 Lille — Tel.: (20) 52 82 40
— Sociéte de développement régional du Nord et du Pas-de-Calais, 108 rue de Jemappes — F-59000 Lille — Tel.: (20) 52 62 80
— Crédit national, 45 rue Saint-Dominique — F-75700 Paris — Tel.: (1) 555 91 10
— Banque populaire de la Loire, 1 Place de l'Hôtel de Ville — F-42007 Saint-Etienne Cedex-Tel.: (77) 33 39 61

ITALY

— Finlombarda, Piazza Belgioioso 2 — I-20121 Milano — Tel.: (02) 70 58 57
— Mediocredito Lombardo, Via Broletto 20 — I-20121 Milano — Tel.: (02) 88 701
— Mediocredito Piemontese, Piazza Solferino 22 — I-10121 Torino — Tel.: (011) 53 47 42

[1] Whose net fixed assets do not exceed 75 million ECU.

— Istituto Mobilare Italiano, Viale dell'Arte 25 — I-00144 Roma — Tel.: (06) 54 501
— Mediocredito Ligure, Via G. d'Annunzio 23, Casella postale 1362 — I-16121 Genoa — Tel.: (010) 53 11 31
— Mediocredito Friuli-Venezia Giulia, Via Acquileia, 1 — I-33100 Udine — Tel.: (0432) 956 51

GRAND DUCHY OF LUXEMBOURG
— Société nationale de crédit et d'investissement, 3, rue de la Congrégation — L-Luxembourg — Tel.: 47 83 15

NETHERLANDS
— De Nationale Investeringsbank, Carnegieplein 4 — NL — Den Haag — Tel.: (70) 46 94 64

ROYAUME-UNI
— Industrial and Commercial Finance Corporation, 91 Waterloo Road — London SE1 8XP — Tel.: (01) 928 7822
— National Westminster Bank PLC (Domestic Banking Division) 41, Lothbury — London EC2P 2 BP — Tel.: (01) 606 6060
— Barclays Bank PLC, 3 Queen Victoria Street — London EC4P 4AT — Tel.: (01) 626 1567
— Cooperative Bank, Balloon Street — Manchester M60 4EP — Tel.: (061) 832 3456
— Scottish Development Agency, 120 Bothwell Street — Glasgow G2 7JP (Scotland) — Tel.: (041) 248 2700
— Clydesdale Bank PLC, 30 St. Vincent Place — Glasgow G1 2HL (Scotland) — Tel.: (041) 248 7070
— Welsh Development Agency, Pontypridd Midglamorgan CF37 5UT — Tel.: (044385) 2666
— The Royal Bank of Scotland PLC, 42 St. Andrew Square PO Box 31 — Edinburgh EH2 2YE — Tel.: (031) 556 8555

More detailed information on ECSC conversion loans may be obtained from the competent national departments, the intermediaries mentioned, the local consultants of the Commission of the European Communities and the following departments: DG XVI, Division B3, 200 rue de la Loi, B-1049 Brussels, Tel. (02) 235 34 20; DG XVIII, Directorate B, Bâtiment Jean Monnet, L-2920 Luxembourg, Tel. 4301 3226.

Workers' housing (Article 54)

Eligibility and selection criteria

The construction, purchase and modernization of housing for the personnel of the ECSC industries are eligible; the housing may be for rent or owner-occupied. In its guidelines of 30 November 1979 for the execution of the ninth workers' housing programme 1979-83, the Commission has decided to accord priority to operations which help to attain the sectoral objectives of the Community and which improve the living conditions of the workers.

Financial provisions

A further amount of 30 million ECU has been allocated to the second instalment of the ninth programme. The financial institutions or the ECSC undertakings themselves act as intermediaries. Loans are generally granted for 20 to 25 years at an interest rate of 1% plus the administration costs of the intermediaries. Loans are always paid in national currency. Supplementary loans may be granted on request in any currency, at the normal capital market rate.

Procedures

Generally, applications are submitted by the persons concerned to their employers. Applications are then centralized by regional committees on which management and unions are equally represented. The committees submit financing proposals and the Commission takes the final decision.

(4) Grants towards occupational redeployment and social measures to assist former ECSC workers (Article 56 (2) (b)

Eligibility and selection criteria

The ECSC makes grants to the Member States to assist ECSC workers [1] affected by changes in conditions on the coal and steel markets. The grants can be used for the occupational redeployment of former ECSC workers in the form of:

(i) income support: tideover allowances in the event of unemployment, severance payment, aid towards early retirement, compensation for loss of pay (in the event of a change of activity or new job);

(ii) mobility aid: travel costs, removal expenses, resettlement allowances, separation allowances;

(iii) aid towards the vocational training of workers having to change employment: operating expenses, equipment expenses, premiums or income supplements for workers in training; and re-employment premiums.

Aid is granted either under bilateral agreements concluded between the Commission and the Member States, or under 'social measures' — multiannual special financing programmes authorized by the Council.

A grant is conditional upon payment by the Member State of an amount at least equal (except in certain cases) to the ECSC contribution.

Financial provisions

The grant of aid is negotiated between the Commission and the Member State concerned; the amount depends on the needs and problems of the individual Member State.

The bilateral agreements between the Commission and the Member States constitute a commitment by the Commission to contribute towards certain benefits granted to workers made redundant from the coal and steel industries, whatever the number of persons entitled to such benefits. The grants, which the Commission makes in the various Member States are essentially similar in form, and generally 50% of the cost to public funds over and above the grants or allowances under general social security or occupational redeployment schemes.

Grants under the 'social measures' are paid out of resources specifically allocated for this purpose and authorized in successive instalments. Appropriations are granted on the basis of expenditure estimated by the Member States, but within the limit of the maximum amount of resources available.

Procedures

Applications must be submitted to the Commission by the national authorities (generally the Ministry of Labour and Employment or the Ministry of Industry).

---

[1] Workers producing ECSC products within the meaning of Annexes I, II and III to the ECSC Treaty are considered to be ECSC workers.

5. Technical and economic research (Article 55)

Eligibility and selection criteria

For scientific and technical research in the coal and steel industries, financial assistance is provided to cover expenditure directly incurred for research purposes, including staffing, equipment and operating expenses.

The Commission may also grant financial support for pilot and demonstration projects in the iron and steel industry that will permit the transition to industrial and commercial exploitation of production techniques, processes and plant and products that are innovatory in themselves or in their applications and for which major capital expenditure is required to establish technical and/or commercial feasibility. The projects must offer prospects of economic viability demonstrated by previous studies and research.

Aid for social and medical research takes the form of a contribution to staffing costs or the cost of research equipment. The priority research subjects are published in the Official Journal under the new guidelines for research programmes.

Financial provisions

As a rule, aid granted for technical research in the coal and steel industries is equivalent to 60% of expenditure. However, in the case of pilot and/or demonstration projects, the Community's financial support may not normally exceed 50% of the total cost of the project. Aid for social and medical research is determined on a case-by-case basis.

Procedures

Aid for technical research relating to coal and steel may be granted to any undertaking, research centre or institute, or individual, even if they are not directly connected with coal-mining or the iron and steel industry. Applications for financial aid should be sent to the Commission of the European Communities by 1 September. Official Journal C 159 of 24. 6. 1982 contains fuller details on the applications procedure.

For pilot and/or demonstration projects in the iron and steel industry, applications for financial aid from any undertaking, research institute or other body having an activity related to iron and steel are to be sent, before 1 February of each year, to:

Commission of the European Communities,
Directorate-General for Science, Research and Development,
Iron and Steel Pilot/Demonstration Projects,
200 rue de la Loi,
B-1049 Brussels.

After consulting the Consultative Committee and obtaining the assent of the Council[1], the Commission of the European Communities takes its decision on the granting of financial aid. In the case of pilot and/or demonstration projects, the Commission takes its decision after consulting a committee of qualified experts. If the decision is positive, the Commission of the European Communities implements it by concluding with the beneficiary a contract which lays down the amount of aid and the conditions on which it is granted.

---

[1] Research forming part of a general programme which has itself received the Council's assent after consultation of the Consultative Committee is exempt from these procedures.

Official Journal C 81 of 24. 3. 1983 contains fuller details on the conditions and arrangements for granting financial aids for pilot and/or demonstration projects in the iron and steel industry.

For grants for social and medical research, the beneficiaries are selected by one of the following methods, depending on the type of project:

(i) the Commission makes direct contact with the firms or research institutes and centres which it hopes will participate; or

(ii) the Commission publishes an invitation to submit proposals to which any interested institute may reply.

Applications to be sent direct to the Commission of the European Communities, must contain a detailed programme and supply the following information:

(i) the aim of the research and the results expected,

(ii) financing: funds available, amount of aid requested,

(iii) legal status of the applicant,

(iv) research programme: means of execution and estimated costs.

(6) Studies on possibilities for re-employing redundant ECSC workers (Article 46(4))

Aim

Under Article 46 of the ECSC Treaty, the European Coal and Steel Community may at any time consult governments, the various parties concerned (undertakings, workers, consumers and dealers) and their associations, and any experts. The various parties concerned and their associations are entitled to present any suggestions or comments on questions affecting them, and it is in response to these that certain studies and surveys are carried out. The ECSC shall also take part, at the request of the governments concerned, in studying the possibilities for re-employing, in existing industries or through the creation of new activities, workers made redundant by market developments or technical changes (paragraph 4).

Eligibility and selection criteria

Studies carried out under Article 46 (1), (2), (3) and (5) are financed on the initiative of the Commission of the European Communities, but under Article 46 (4) the Member States may request the Commission's financial assistance for studies concerning the diversification of economic activities permitting the re-employment of former ECSC workers.

In order to reinforce conversion policy in the regions affected by industrial restructuring, studies and measures relating to small new activity projects are carried out under Article 46 (Article 774 of the Community budget).

Financial provisions

The Commission generally contributes 50% of the cost of such studies.

Procedures

Member States should send applications to:

Commission of the European Communities,
Directorate-General for Regional Policy,
200 rue de la Loi,
B-1049 Brussels.
Tel. 235 1667;
Telex: 21877 COMEU B

(7) Coking coal and coke for the iron and steel industry (Article 95 and Decision 73/287/ECSC as last amended by Decision 84/759/ECSC)

Aim

This is a special system for supplies to the steel industry introduced in 1967 within the framework of the Community coal policy.
The system allows Member States to grant production aid where the cost price of Community coal exceeds the price of coal imported from non-member countries. This national production aid may possible be supplemented by a marketing aid for deliveries to areas remote from the coalfield or to other countries.

Financial provisions

The system also allows selling prices to be aligned on world prices, even where there is no actual competition from coal or coke from non-member countries at the point of consumption.

In the case of intra-Community trade, marketing aid may be reimbursed by a Community fund. The rate (variable according to the location of the blast furnace) is 5.10 ECU per tonne for deliveries supplied direct by sea and 3.10 ECU in other cases. Community financing arrangements cover an annual quantity of coal amounting to no more than 10 million tonnes, 159/84 ECSC Article (2).

Procedures

In order to ensure that this mechanism is applied in a Community-minded way, and/that certain limits are respected, the Commission periodically publishes indicator prices which are the lower limit for calculating production aids in the four Member States concerned (Belgium, France, Federal Republic of Germany, United Kingdom) and alignments for all transactions relating to Community coal or coke.

TABLE V

Description	Legal basis ECSC Treaty
A – Loans	
1. Industrial loans:	Article 54
(i) to facilitate carrying out investment programmes	1st paragraph
(ii) to assist the financing of works and installations which contribute directly and primarily to increasing the production, reducing the production costs or facilitating the marketing of products	2nd paragraph
2. Conversion loans	Article 56 (1)(b) and (2)(a)
3. Loans for building ECSC workers' housing	Article 54
B – Interest rebates on ECSC loans	
4. These interest rebates are granted on:	Article 54, 2nd paragraph (industrial loans)
(i) ECSC-industrial loans for: security, hygiene, anti-pollution measures, multinational investment or investment intended to reduce bottlenecks at Community level or to establish research or training centres	Commission Communications: OJ C 73, 18. 6. 1970 OJ C 146, 25. 11. 1974
(ii) ECSC industrial loans for investment projects concerning coal production	Commission Communication: OJ C 79, 29. 3. 1980
(iii) ECSC industrial loans for investment projects to promote the consumption of Community coal	Commission Communication: OJ C 343, 31. 12. 1982
5. And on:	Article 56 (1) (b) and (2) (a) (conversion loans)
Conversion loans (direct loans, and indirect loans through the intermediary of financial institutions)	Commission Communication: OJ C 191, 16. 7. 1983
C – Redeployment aids and social aid	
6. Redeployment aids	Article 56 (1) (c) and 2 (b)
(i) allowances to undertakings to enable them to continue paying such of their workers as may have to be temporarily laid off as a result of the undertakings' change of activity	
(ii) resettlement allowances to workers	
(iii) the financing of vocational retraining for workers having to change their employment	
7. Social measures accompanying the restructuring of the coal and steel industries: (i) early retirement (ii) short-time working (iii) measures to provide new jobs	Article 56 (2) (b) Council Decision 82/164/EEC of 23. 2. 1982 OJ L 74, 18. 3. 1982 Council Decision 82/652/EEC of 21. 9. 1982 OJ L 277, 29. 9. 1982 Council Decision 84/384/EEC of 23. 7. 1984 OJ L 208, 3. 8. 1984

Description	Legal basis ECSC Treaty
8. Aid towards the financing of studies on the possibilities for re-employing redundant ECSC workers	Article 46
D – for research	
9. Promotion of technical and economic research relating to:	Article 55
(i) the production and increased use of coal and steel	Commission Communications: Applications for and the grant of financial aids for technical, economic and social research OJ C 159, 24. 6. 1982
(ii) the production and increased use of coal	Medium-term guidelines for technical coal research (1981-85) OJ C 94, 17. 4. 1980
(iii) the production and increased use of steel	Medium-term orientation for steel research in relation to the general objectives for steel (1981-85) OJ C 99, 2. 5. 1981
(iv) safety and industrial hygiene in the ECSC industries	Fourth ECSC medical research programme - Effects on the health of workers of physical and other occupational factors at the workplace OJ C 307, 27. 11. 1981 Establishment of a second research programme - 'Safety in Mining' OJ C 195, 29. 7. 1982 Fifth research programme 'Industrial Hygiene in Mines' OJ C 332, 8. 12. 1983
10. Pilot and/or demonstration projects in the iron and steel industry	The granting of financial support for 'pilot' and/or 'demonstration' projects OJ C 81, 24. 4. 1983
E – Market support	
11. Aids for intra-Community trade in coking coal and coke for the iron and steel industry	Article 95 and Decision 73/287/ECSC as last amended by Decision 759/84/ECSC.

Chapter VI: Specific measures for the energy sector

Euratom investment loans

Aim

The purpose of Euratom loans is to promote the use of nuclear energy in order to reduce the Community's overdependence on external energy supplies.

The Commission is empowered to issue loans, on behalf of the European Atomic Energy Community (Euratom), the proceeds of which are lent for the purpose of financing investment projects relating to the industrial production of electricity in nuclear power stations and to industrial fuel cycle installations.

The Euratom borrowing and lending mechanism provides more ample credit facilities for electricity producers facing a substantial increase in their investment and operating expenditure.

Eligibility and selection criteria

The investment projects eligible are those relating to the industrial production of electricity in nuclear power stations and to industrial fuel cycle installations.

Preference is given to projects which ensure the most profitable conditions and which relate to installations of optimum size.

Financial provisions

Loans normally cover not more than 20% of the total investment cost.

The Commission finances its loans by means of funds borrowed on the basis of the loan applications which it receives. The Commission administers the borrowed funds, while the loans are administered by the Commission in collaboration with the European Investment Bank. The terms of loans depend on those ruling on the financial markets. Borrowing transactions and the lending transactions related thereto are expressed in the same currency. The costs incurred by the Community in concluding and carrying out each transaction are borne by the beneficiary undertakings.

Loans are guaranteed in the manner customary in banking practice.

Procedures

Firms interested should send applications to:

Commission of the European Communities
Directorate-General for Credit and Investments
Jean Monnet Building
L-2719 Luxembourg
Tel. 43011, Tlx 2331

TABLE VI

Specific energy measures: Euratom loans and other measures

A – Euratom loans

Legal basis	OJ	Date	Description
1. Basic Decision 77/270/Euratom Amending Decision 82/170/Euratom	L 88 L 78	6. 4. 1977 24. 3. 1982	Financing investment projects relating to the industrial production of electricity in nuclear power stations and to industrial fuel cycle installations.

B – Other measures

Legal basis	OJ	Date	Description
2. Regulation 3056/73	L 312	13. 11. 1973	Technological development in the hydrocarbons sector
3. Regulation 1971/83, mended by Regulation 2125/84	L 195 L 196	19. 7. 1983 26. 7. 1984	Financial support for pilot industrial projects and demonstration projects relating to the liquefaction and gasification of solid fuels.
4. Regulation 1972/83 mended by Regulation 2126/84	L 195 L 196	19. 7. 1983 26. 7. 1984	Financial support for demonstration projects relating to the exploitation of alternative energy sources and to energy saving and the substitution of hydrocarbons.

Technological development in the hydrocarbons sector (Council Regulation (EEC) No 3056/73)).

Aim

To promote projects of technological development directly associated with prospecting for, extracting, storing or transporting oil and gas which are likely to improve the Community's availability of supplies.

Eligibility and selection criteria

Community projects considered of prime importance in securing supplies of oil and natural gas may qualify for financial aid.

Financial provisions

The main forms for aid are:

(i) aids which are repayable under certain conditions. Community aid has been given mainly in the form of grants, amounting to 25-40% of total costs;

(ii) loans or loan guarantees for projects.

The type and volume of aid is fixed with regard to its effect in improving the hydrocarbon supply conditions.

Procedures

Any natural or legal person (firm or group of firms) may be granted aid. The Commission publishes each year in invitation for the submission of projects; the last invitation was published in Official Journal C 208 of 8. 8. 1984. Applications should be sent direct to:

Commission of the European Communities
Directorate-General for Energy
200 rue de la Loi
B-1040 Brussels

Liquefaction and gasification of solid fuels (Council Regulation (EEC) No 1971/83 as amended by Council Regulation No 2125/84).

Aim

The conversion of solid fuels into gaseous and liquid products represents an alternative energy source which, after it has been developed to the industrial stage, could improve energy supply conditions in the Community by contributing towards diversification.

Main features

The Community may grant financial support for pilot industrial projects and demonstration projects relating to the liquefaction and gasification of solid fuels.

A 'pilot industrial installation' means an installation having adequate capacity and using components which are large enough to increase the reliability of the economic and technical data needed to progress from the research and development stage to the demonstration stage and, in certain cases, directly to the industrial and commercial stages.

'Demonstration' means operating an installation so as to make it possible to collect all the data on technical and economic viability and to proceed with the least risk to industrial and commercial exploitation of the technology.

Community aid is governed by Council Regulation (EEC) No 1971/83[1] as amended by Regulation (EEC) No 2125/84[2].

Eligibility and selection criteria

The detailed list of the three fields of application eligible for Community assistance is given in the Annex to the regulation; the three fields are gasification (according to by-products), underground gasification and liquefaction (according to processes).

All projects must satisfy the following conditions:

(a) must relate to the creation of pilot industrial installations or demonstration installations;

(b) must implement techniques or processes which are innovatory in themselves or in their application;

---

[1] OJ L 195, 19. 7. 1983.

[2] OJ L 196, 26. 7. 1984.

(c) they must be likely to increase the technical and economic reliability of the process and have a reference character;

(d) they must present difficulties with regard to finance because of the considerable technical and economic risks involved to the extent that they would very probably not be carried out without public and/or Community financial support;

(e) they should, in principle, be carried out within the territory of the Community.

Financial provisions

The Community's financial support may not exceed 49% of the eligible cost of the project. The level of support is determined for each project individually. Half of the Community contribution is repayable under certain conditions in the case of demonstration projects. Community aid for pilot industrial projects is not repayable.

Procedures

Projects and applications for Community assistance are to be sent direct to the Commission in answer to an invitation to submit projects published in the *Official Journal of the European Communities.* The notice published in the Official Journal states the information to be provided in support of the aid application.

The Commission decides whether to grant or refuse financial support for each project submitted, and then negotiates and concludes the contracts with the persons responsible for executing the projects. To that end it draws up model contracts, available on request, setting forth the rights and obligations of each party, including the procedures for any repayment of financial support granted and for access to and dissemination of expertise.

Exploitation of alternative energy sources, energy saving and the substitution of hydrocarbons (Council Regulation (EEC) No 1972/83 as amended by Council Regulation (EEC) No 2126/84)

Aim

In order to enable investment in alternatives to oil as an energy source and in the more rational use of energy, the Community is pursuing research, development and demonstration policies. One of the methods used by these policies is the financial support for innovatory demonstration projects aimed at improving energy efficiency and making use of alternatives to hydrocarbons as energy sources.

Main characteristics

The Community's financial support is granted for demonstration projects in the following fields:

(a) alternative energy sources; projects to exploit any potential source of energy except nuclear energy;

(b) energy saving; projects for a significant improvement energy efficiency;

(c) hydrocarbons substitution; projects for the use of non-renewable energy sources instead of liquid or gaseous hydrocarbons, without leading to a significant increase in primary energy consumption.

The conditions for Community aid are laid down in Council Regulation (EEC) No 1972/83[1] as amended by Regulation (EEC) No 2126/84[2].

---

[1] OJ L 195, 19. 7. 1983.
[2] OJ L 196, 26. 7. 1984.

Eligibility and selection criteria

The detailed list of the fields of application eligible for Community aid is given in Annexes to the regulation. For alternative energy sources, the fields of application are the following geothermal energy, solar energy, biomass, wind and ocean energy and hydro-electric power.

For energy saving, the fields of application are grouped under four headings: buildings; supply and use of process heat and of electricity in industry and in agriculture; energy industry and transport. Lastly for the hydrocarbons substitution, the applications are solid fuels, the use of electric power and heat transmission, distribution and storage.

All demonstration projects must satisfy the following conditions:

(a) they must relate to the creation of full-size installations for the exploitation of alternative sources or energy conservation or hydrocarbons substitution in significant quantities;

(b) they must exploit innovatory techniques, processes or products or a new application of techniques, processes or products which are already known and whose research and development stage is considered to be over;

(c) they must be likely to encourage the construction of other installations of the same type;

(d) they must offer promising prospects of industrial and commercial viability as shown by prior studies and research;

(e) they must present difficulties with regard to finance because of the considerable technical and economic risks involved, to the extent that they would very probably not be carried out without public and/or Community financial support;

(f) they should, in principle, be carried out within the territory of the Community.

Financial provisions

The Community's financial support may not exceed 49% of the eligible cost of the project. The level of support is determined for each project individually. Half of the Community contribution is repayable under certain conditions.

Procedures

The procedures are the same as for projects relating to the liquefaction and gasification of solid fuels.

Chapter VII — Specific aids for transport infrastructure

Aim

By means of the specific measure in the field of transport infrastructure, the Community wishes to contribute to the harmonious development of a balanced infrastructure network and to its socio-economic benefit for the Community.

Main features

The purpose of the Community's specific measure is:

(i) to eliminate notorious bottlenecks within the Community or straddling its external frontiers; or

(ii) to improve major traffic links between all Member States.

A special financial effort is made to modernize the main transport routes in Greece.

Eligibility and selection criteria

Hitherto, projects financed by the Community have for the most part been directly proposed to the Council by the Commission. However, certain frontier infrastructures depend on a direct choice by the Commission.

Eligible projects must satisfy a number of criteria directly linked to their Community interest bottlenecks within the Community, major traffic links between Member States, etc.).

TABLE VII

Specific aids for transport infrastructure

Legal basis	OJ	Date	Description
Regulation (EEC) No 3620/84	L 333	21. 12. 1984	Specific measure in the field of transport infrastructure

Financial conditions

The financial support granted by the Community may not exceed 25% of the total cost of each project or of the particular stage of the project to be supported.

Under no circumstances may contributions from all Community sources exceed 50% of the total cost of a given project.

Procedures

The major transport infrastructures eligible for Community assistance are selected by the Commission and proposed to the Council, with the exception of certain frontier infrastructures for which the Commission takes the aid decision directly.

In this case, Member States send projects to the Commission; the Commission consults the Committee on Transport Infrastructures consisting of representatives of the Member States, takes a decision and notifies the Council thereof.

Within 30 days of this notification, any Member State may refer the matter to the Council. The Council, acting on a qualified majority, may take a different decision within 45 days. If the matter is not referred to the Council by any Member State, or if the Council does not act within the above period of time, the decision of the Commission becomes final.

Chapter VIII: Action by the Community relating to the environment

Aim

The purpose of action by the Community relating to the environment is to ensure a preventive reduction in pollution and a more careful use of natural resources in the most economically sensible fashion, to improve the techniques and methods for monitoring the quality of the natural environment, and to make a contribution towards the maintenance and re-establishment of seriously threatened biotopes.

Main features

Action by the Community relating to the environment, established by Council Regulation (EEC) No 1872/84[1], concerns three fields of application:

(a) demonstration projects aimed at developing new 'clean' technologies, i. e. technologies which cause little or no pollution and which may also be more economical in the use of natural resources, in specific areas;

(b) demonstration projects aimed at developing new techniques and methods for measuring and monitoring the quality of the natural environment;

(c) projects providing an incentive and aimed at contributing towards the maintenance or re-establisment of seriously threatened biotopes which are the habitat of endangered species and are of particular importance to the Community, under Directive 79/409/EEC.

Eligibility and selection criteria

To be eligible for financial support, a project must be of interest to the Community and in terms of protection of the environment and/or the management of natural resources.

Projects which fall within other Community programmes are not eligible. Demonstration projects aimed at developing new 'clean' technologies must fall within the following areas: surface treatments (scouring, lacquering, galvanizing and cadmium-plating processes, replacement of cadmium), leather industry, textile industry, cellulose and paper industries, mining and quarrying, chemical industry and agri-food industries. These projects must also:

(a) implement innovatory technologies or procedures for which the research phase may be assumed to have been completed but which are still untested or not yet in existence in the Community;

(b) by their demonstration value, be such as to encourage the creation of other similar installations which are capable of noticeably reducing adverse effects on the environment;

(c) first and foremost concern installations or procedures which, either because of the large amounts or the particularly dangerous nature of their emissions, seriously harm the environment, while at the same time a reduction in the use of natural resources should be aimed at.

Demonstration projects aimed at developing new techniques and methods for measuring and monitoring the quality of the natural environment must cover first and foremost the major air, water and soil pollutants and contribute towards harmonization of methods of measurement and comparability of measurement results obtained within the Community.

---

[1] OJ L 176, 3. 7. 1984.

TABLE VIII

Legal basis	OJ	Date	Description
Regulation (EEC) No 1872/84	L 176	3. 7. 1984	Action by the Community relating to the environment
1. Article 1(a)			new 'clean' technologies
2. Article 1(b)			measuring and monitoring techniques
3. Article 1(c)			maintenance or re-establishment of biotopes

Financial support for projects relating to biotopes shall be commensurate with the importance of the area to the Community and with the urgency of the need for the financial support in question.

Financial provisions

Community financial support may not exceed:

(i) 30% of the cost of demonstration projects relating to new 'clean' technologies and to new techniques and methods for measuring and monitoring;

(ii) 50% of the cost of the projects aimed at contributing towards the maintenance or re-establishment of seriously threatened biotopes.

In the event of commercial exploitation of the results of a project, the Community may request repayments of its financial contribution.

Procedures

Financial support under the regulation may be granted to the natural persons, or the legal persons constituted in accordance with the law of the Member States, who are responsible for the project.

Applications for financial support for demonstration projects relating to new 'clean' technologies and to new techniques and methods for measuring and monitoring the quality of the natural environment must be drawn up in response to an invitation to submit projects prepared by the Commission and published in the *Official Journal of the European Communities*.

The invitation to submit projects specifies the particulars to be provided in accordance with Regulation No 1872/84 (Annex II). Applications are to be sent to the Commission with copies to the competent authorities of the Member State concerned.

Applications for financial support for projects concerning biotopes are to be sent to the Commission through the intermediary of the Member States; they must contain the particulars specified in Annex III to Regulation No 1872/84.

After the Commission has decided whether to grant or refuse financial support for eligible projects, the obligations deriving from Community support are laid down in contracts concluded between the Commission and the persons responsible for the projects.

Recipients of Community financial support must send the Commission, each year or at its request, a report on the fulfilment of the contractual obligations towards the Commission, and in particular on the progress of work on the project and the expenditure incurred in carrying it out.

Chapter IX: Measures relating to research and innovation

A. Measures relating to research (see Table IX-A)

Aim

The main aims of Community research policy are as follows:

(i) promoting competitiveness in industry, agriculture and fisheries,

(ii) improving the management of raw materials,

(iii) improving the management of energy resources,

(iv) stepping up development aid,

(v) improving living and working conditions,

(vi) stimulating the efficacy of the Community's scientific and technical potential.

Community research activities are conducted essentially at three levels with different amounts of Community financial aid:

(i) at the Joint Research Centre,

(ii) by contract research involving financial contributions from the contractor,

(iii) through coordination of Member States' research activities.

This booklet merely gives the general rules governing contract research and a more detailed description of three programmes. Fuller information is given in the *Vade-mecum of contract research* (Office for Official Publications of the European Communities, 1984).

Eligibility and selection criteria for contract research

Any natural or legal person established within the Community may be eligible. Besides the scientific and economic significance of a project for the European Community, the main selection criteria for research proposals are the scientific competence of the applicant, the originality of the research work proposed, the feasibility in scientific technical and terms and the applicant's financial contribution to the overall cost.

Financial provisions

As a rule, the Community's contribution does not exceed 50% of the total cost of the project. In certain exceptional cases, it may be increased to a higher rate. Provision can be made for 100% financial participation if the Commission has an exclusive interest in the project concerned.

Procedures

When research programmes have been adopted by the Council, invitations to submit proposals for the entire programme or parts of it are published in the 'C' series of the *Official Journal of the European Communities*.

The research and development proposals must relate to the areas specified in the invitations. The proposals are assessed confidentially to protect the commercial interests of the applicant.

Further information may obtained from:

Commission of the European Communities
Directorate-General XII, Science, Research and Development
Rue de la Loi 200
B-1049 Brussels - Tel. 235 1111

Since it would not possible in this booklet to give an exhaustive description of all the research areas eligible for Community grants, we will confine ourselves to three programmes where the detailed rules differ most from the general rules described above.

These are the programmes relating to the environment, the programme to stimulate the efficacy of the Community's scientific and technical potential and the programme for research and development in information technologies (Esprit).

Sectoral research and development programme in the field of environment (environmental protection and climatology) — indirect and concerted actions (Council Decision 81/213/EEC as amended by Council Decision 84/139/EEC)

Aim

The scientific and technical data obtained through this research are to be made available as support for the environmental action programme.

The programme attaches great importance to the prevention of environmental pollution through the use of 'clean' technologies and to the increasingly important questions relating to the management of waste, including toxic waste. Greater attention also needs to be paid to the preservation and the protection of the rural environment, preservation of wild animals and plants and the improvement of living conditions and the quality of life.

Eligibility and selection criteria

(The research projects to be conducted as part of the concerted actions are not included here).

The programme provides for the co-financing of research projects in the following areas:

Sub-programme I 'environment protection'

(i) sources, pathways and effects of pollutants,

(ii) reduction and prevention of pollution and nuisances,

(iii) protection, conservation and management of natural environements,

(iv) environment information management,

(v) man-environment interactions: development of methods;

Sub-programme II 'climatology'

(i) understanding climate,

(ii) man-climate interactions.

Projects may be proposed by companies, including small and medium-sized businesses, universities and other bodies established within the Community.

Financial provisions

The Community's financial contribution normally covers up to 50% of the cost of the project. In exceptional cases, this rule may be waived.

Procedures

Projects are submitted in response to a call for proposals published in the *Official Journal of the European Communities*. Requests for information should be adressed to:

Commission of the European Communities
Directorate for Science, Research and Development
Joint Research Centre
rue de la Loi 200
B-1049 Brussels.

Experimental action to stimulate the efficacy of the Community's scientific and technical potential (Council Decision 83/331/EEC)

Aim

The stimulation plan has three aims:

(i) to encourage the mobility of researchers and communication between scientists,

(ii) to develop scientific and technical cooperation,

(iii) to promote the placing of young researchers in employment.

Eligibility and selection criteria

Three kinds of activity are to be given priority support:

(i) activities for which the joining up of research teams working in different Member States is beneficial or indispensable,

(ii) activities enabling the promotion of high-quality teams which, because of the novel nature of their work, do not yet benefit from the support which their worth, and the potential value of work, would seem to justify,

(iii) activities leading to a strengthening of the communication and diffusion of information within the scientific and technical system.

These activities concern, in the main, the following seven areas:

pharmacobiology,

solid-state physics,

optics,

combustion,

photometry/photoacoustic,

climatology

interface phenomena.

To be accepted, the activities must be multinational in character.

Financial provisions

The Commission may provide research allocations, grants to help laboratory twinning and grants to assist research teams, seminars and courses. The Commission may also conclude development contracts with research teams.

Procedures

Proposals are submitted in response to a call for proposals published in the 'C' series the *Official Journal of the European Communities*. Requests for information should be sent to:

Commission of the European Communities
Directorate-General for Science, Research and Development
Rue de la loi 200
B-1049 Brussels.

Research and development in information technologies (Esprit) (Council Decisions 84/130/EEC and 84/157/EEC)

Aim

The overall aim of Esprit is to create or consolidate European industrial potential in information technologies. In order to achieve this aim, the Esprit programme promotes research and development cooperation between Community firms, university institutes and research centres and contributes to the dissemination of results obtained.

Eligibility and selection criteria

The programme provides for the co-financing of precompetitive research and development activities in five areas:

microelectronics,

software technology,

advanced information processing,

office systems,

computer integrated manufacture.

The activities must fall within the working programme adopted each year by the Council. They may be proposed by companies, including small and medium-sized businesses, universities and other bodies established within the Community. The activities must normally involve the participation of at least two associated independent bodies, which must not be established within one and the same Member State.

Financial provisions

The Community's financial support normally covers up to 50% of the cost of the project. In exceptional cases, this rule may be waived.

Procedures

Projects are normally submitted in response to a call for proposals published in the *Official Journal of the European Communities*. Further information may be obtained from:

Commission of the European Communities
Information and telelcommunications technologies task force
(Attention: Esprit)
Rue de la Loi 200
B-1040 Brussels.

B. Measures relating to industry and innovation (see Table IX-B)

The main aim of these measures is to improve the competitiveness of Community industry, notably by boosting the development of new technologies and by creating a European framework favouring industrial innovation.

Community support mechanism in the field of data processing (Council Regulation (EEC) No 1996/79, and Council Decision 79/783/EEC as amended by Council Decision 84/254/EEC

Aim

The aim of the support mechanism is to encourage cooperation between undertakings and users in different Member States in the area of data processing development.

Eligibility and selection criteria

Financial support may be granted to feasibility studies, predevelopment studies, development projects and pilot projects stemming from users or undertakings in at least two Member States, including associations of undertakings comprising at least two undertakings established in different Member States. Projects of Community interest proposed by the Commission may also be financed.

The projects must fall within the multiannual programme adopted by the Council in Decision 79/783/EEC (OJ L 231, 13. 9. 1979, p. 23) as amended by Council Decision 84/254/EEC (OJ L 126, 12. 5. 1984, p. 27).

Financial provisions

Financial support may be granted in the form of:

(i) loans covering up to 50% of the total cost of predevelopment studies, development projects and pilot projects stemming from undertakings or users,

(ii) grants covering up to 100% of the total cost with a ceiling of 100 000 ECU in the case of feasibility studies,

(iii) grants or loans covering up to 100% of the total cost of projects and studies launched on the Commission's initiative.

The loans are granted on terms and for a duration which are fixed on the basis of the particular features of the project. The loans may be granted without interest for all or part of their duration.

The Commission may defer or cancel the payments outstanding if the results obtained differ substantially from those envisaged when the contract was concluded. Due dates may also be postponed if commercial exploitation is delayed. If the work does not result in commercial exploitation within a five-year period, the Commission may release the beneficiaries from their obligation to repay the loan.

Procedures

Projects are normally submitted in reponse to a call for proposals published in the *Official Journal of the European Communities*. Requests for information should be addressed to:

Commission of the European Communities
Information and telecommunications technologies task force
Rue de la Loi 200
B-1049 Brussels.

Transnational development of the supporting infrastructure for innovation and technology transfer (Council Decision 83/624/EEC)

Aim

The main aim of this programme is to promote the rapid penetration of the Community's economies by new technologies as they become available. The programme comprises a package of measures designed to reinforce national structures intended for this purpose, in particular by adding a European dimension to research exploitation operations, to technology transfer and to specialized advisory and financial services, particularly those intended for small and medium-sized undertakings.

Eligibility and selection criteria

To be eligibile for Community support, projects must fall within the terms of the lists of priority actions drawn up annually by the Commission. The following activities or projects are taken into consideration:

(i) activities or projects involving partners established in different Member States,

(ii) activities or projects involving operations on a Community scale or services open to all Member States,

(iii) programmes for developing innovation infrastructure, particularly for the benefit of Member States with weaker infrastructures.

Action launched include the following:

(i) support for the establishment of transnational collaboration between technology and management advisory services,

(ii) aid intended to confer a European character on conferences and meetings on technology or innovation,

(iii) support for the establishment of European networks of advisory bodies specializing in export services so as to set up pilot projects involving collaboration between innovatory small and medium-sized undertakings wishing to expand into foreign markets.

Financial provisions

The activities or projects undertaken on the Commission's responsibility are financed in full by the Community. Other activities or projects chosen by the Commission qualify for partial Community financing. Contributions are normally limited to an initial launching period or are for a specified duration.

Procedures

Activities or projects are generally submitted in response to calls for proposals published in the *Official Journal of the European Communities.* Requests for information should be addressed to:

Commission of the European Communities
Directorate-General for the Information Market and Innovation
DG XIII/A-2, Office B.4/099
L-2920 Luxembourg.

TABLE IX-B

Legal basis	Description
Regulation (EEC) No 1996/79 and Decision 79/783/EEC (OJ L 231, 13. 9. 1979) as amended by Decision 84/254/EEC (OJ L 126, 12. 5. 1984)	Community support under the multiannual programme in the field of data processing
Decision 83/624/EEC (OJ L 353, 15. 12. 1983)	Plan for the transnational development of the supporting infrastructure for innovation and technology transfer

Chapter X: European Investment Bank loans

Aim

The task of the European Investment Bank, set up by the Treaty of Rome, is to contribute, through its loan and guarantee operations, to the balanced and steady development of the Community. The bulk of its funds is raised on the capital markets; it must employ them as rationally as possible in the interests of the Community.

Main features

The European Investment Bank is non-profit-making; it finances productive infrastructure and investment projects in all secotrs of the economy. The economy policy objectives which EIB loan and guarantee operations must serve are laid down in Article 130 of the Treaty of Rome and spelt out in the statute and the general directives on credit policy adopted by the Board of Governors. In practice, EIB loan and guarantee operations cover:

(i) in the first place, investment projects in the production, infrastructure and energy sectors which contribute to the economic development of less-developed regions;

(ii) investment projects of common interest to several Member States or the Community as a whole and projects for modernizing or converting undertakings or for developing fresh activities.
These latter categories include
  (a) energy projects which help to reduce the Community's dependence on oil imports, such as the development of indigenous resources, the rational use of energy and energy conservation, and diversification of imports;
  (b) projects for modernizing or converting undertakings, specific projects which help to enhance the competitiveness of Community industry by developing or introducing new or advanced technologies, and projects involving close technical and economic cooperation between undertakings in different Member States;
  (c) infrastructure projects of Community interest which contribute to the economic integration of Europe (motorways, railways, waterways and telecommunications likely to improve intra-Community links or which help to achieve Community objectives such as protection of the environment.

TABLE X

EIB loans

Legal basis	Description
1. Art. 130 (a) EEC	financing of projects for developing less-developed regions
2. Art. 130 (b) EEC	financing of projects for modernizing or converting undertakings or for developing fresh activities
3. Art. 130 (c) EEC	financing of projects of common interest to several Member States or benefiting the Community as a whole.

The Bank may grant loans only for investments which contribute to an increase in general economic productivity. It attaches great importance to the economic merits of the projects and to the likely effect on employment.

Financial provisions

The EIB is authorized to finance only part of the cost of a project, complementing the borrower's own funds and credit from other sources. The Bank does not normally lend more than the equivalent of 50% of a project's fixed asset cost.

To facilitate loan management, the Bank prefers to grant loans of more than 2 million ECU per project but it does finance smaller-scale projects by means of global loans to promote investments by small business.

The system is as follows: the EIB grants a global loan to a bank or financial institution. On a proposal from this bank or institution, and with the agreement of the EIB, the amount is then on-lent to assist schemes which satisfy the EIB's criteria.

Individual loans under the global loan system range between 20 000 ECU and 7.5 million ECU. They help to finance investments of a total unit cost that may not exceed 15 million ECU.

Loans are granted for terms set in accordance with the nature of the project and with the depreciation period for the investment to be financed. The term is generally between 7 and 12 years, but may be as much as 20 years for infrastructure projects; the grace period may be from 2 to 5 years.

The Bank offers borrowers the following loan formats:

(i) loans disbursed in several currencies, either in standard mixes, with make-up, term and interest rate all fixed in advance, or in varying mixes tailored to the borrower's preferences and the Bank's holdings;

(ii) loans disbursed in a single currency.

Loans can be disbursed in ECU's, either wholly or as part of a cocktail of currencies.

The EIB's interest rates are determined by the borrowing rates for each of the currencies of disbursement and by the maturity. As the Bank operates on a non-profit-making basis, its lending rates closely follow fluctuations in interest rates on the financial markets where it obtains the bulk of its funds. The rate or rates charged on each loan are generally those in force on the day when the contract is concluded or on the date of disbursement. Loans are disbursed at par.

Capital reimbursements and interest payments are made in the currencies originally received, usually in equal six-monthly instalments. The Bank makes the granting of loans conditional upon the guarantee of a Member State or other first-class security.

Procedures

Enterprises, public authorities or financial institutions wishing to contact the European Investment Bank should apply to its head office or to its external offices:

European Investment Bank

100, boulevard Konrad Adenauer — L-2950 Luxembourg

Representative Office in Brussels: rue de la Loi 227 — B-1040 Brussels

Office for Operations in Italy: Via Sardegna, 38 — I-00187 Rome

Liaison Office for the United Kingdom: 68 Pall Mall — London SW 1Y 5ES

Representative Office in Athens: Ypsilantou 13-15, Kolonaki — 10675 Athens.

The promoter of the investment can also approach the EIB through his usual bank.

Promoters of small or medium-sized investment projects which could qualify for finance from EIB global loans should submit their application to the financial institution acting as intermediary.

Chapter XI — New Community Instrument (NCI)

Aim

The aim of the NCI is to finance, in the form of loans, investment projects which contribute to greater convergence and integration of Member States' economic policies and, through the dissemination of new technology and innovation or by other means, to reinforce the competitiveness of the Community economy (basic Council Decision 83/200/EEC). In 1983 it was empowered to contract loans totalling 3 000 million ECU, the loans being activited in tranches.

Eligibility criteria

The loans granted from NCI resources must comply with the guidelines laid down by the Council, on the basis of which the Commission decides whether or not projects are eligible.

The guidelines are set out in the authorizations for the issue of loan tranches.

For the tranche covered by the Council's most recent implementing Decision 84/383/EEC decisions on whether or not projects are eligible are taken in accordance with the following guidelines and priorities:

(i) investment projects, mainly those of small and medium-sized undertakings, in industry and directly allied services, which are designed in particular to promote the dissemination of innovation and new technology and which will contribute directly or indirectly to job creation;

(ii) the rational use of energy, the subsitution of other energy sources for oil in all sectors and infrastructure projects facilitating such substitution;

(iii) infrastructure projects which are associated with the development of productive activities, which contribute to regional development or which are of Community interest, such as telecommunications, including information technology, and transport, including the transmission of energy.

The projects and their execution must comply with the provisions of the Treaty and of secondary legislation, in particular those relating to competition, and with Community rules and policies in the fields in question.

TABLE XI

New Community Instrument

Legal basis	OJ	Description
Dec. 83/200/EEC	L 112 28. 4. 1983	Basic decision empowering the Commission to contract loans under the NCI for the purpose of promoting investment within the Community;
Dec. 83/308/EEC	L 164 23. 6. 1983	Implementing decisions for the financing of investment projects in the following sectors:
Dec. 84/383/EEC	L 208 3. 8. 1984	a) investment projects, mainly those small businesses, in industry and directly allied services; b) rational use of energy; c) infrastructure projects which contribute to regional development or are of Community interest.

Financial provisions

After consulting the European Parliament, the Council, acting by a qualified majority on a proposal from the Commission, authorizes the loan tranches and lays down the guidelines for the eligibility of projects.

The Commission raises the necessary recources by borrowing on the capital markets on behalf of the European Economic Community; the borrowings are guaranteed by the general Community budget.

The Commission negotiates the borrowing operations and deposits the funds raised with the European Investment Bank, to be invested on a temporary basis if necessary. Borrowing and lending transactions do not entail any expenditure under the Community budget.

The EIB has received a mandate to administer NCI loans for the account and at the risk of the Community. Interest rates are determined by the rates of the borrowings for each currency of disbursement. NCI loans may, within certain limits, be combined with EIB loans.

Procedures

The implementing decisions for each tranche of borrowings specify the sectors in which the funds are to be lent and lay down the guidelines.

Loan applications are transmitted simultaneously to the Commission and to the EIB.

The Commission decides whether projects are eligible. Where the Commission gives a favourable decision, the EIB decides whether and on what terms to grant the loans, in accordance with its usual criteria and with the procedures laid down in its statute.

The Commission and the EIB sign the loan contracts for the Community.

Chapter XII — Special measures

A. Exceptional Community measure to promote urban renewal in Northern Ireland (Belfast) (Council Regulation (EEC) No 1739/83.

Aim

The aim of this measure is to contribute — together with all the Community measures undertaken in Northern Ireland to the efforts needed to bring about a steady improvement of the situation in the region.

Main features

The measure; which applies for a period of three years (1983-85), consists of the joint financing, by the Community and the public authorities in Northern Ireland, of infrastructure investment projects contributing to urban renewal in the Belfast area.

The total amount of finance to be provided by the Community is 100 million ECU over three years.

Eligibility and selection criteria

The infrastructure projects which the Community may help to finance are chosen from a list to be submitted each year by the United Kingdom,

In order to qualify for a Community contribution, infrastructure projects must satisfy the following conditions:

(i) they must not have been completed at the time the list presented by the United Kingdom is submitted,

(ii) they must involve capital expenditure borne by the public authorities,

(iii) they must contribute to urban renewal in the Belfast area, to the raising of the living standards of the population and to the improvement of the environment,

(iv) they must come within the following categories:

1. leisure, recreation and community facilities;
2. social welfare and health facilities;
3. tourist amenities;
4. land reclamation;
5. industrial zones;
6. harbour facilities;
7. public utility infrastructures;
8. transportation networks;
9. urban drainage;
10. environmental improvements.

(v) they must be consistent with the regional development programme for Northern Ireland.

The United Kingdom Government must also provide the Commission with all the information it needs to satisfy itself that the Community aid is additional to the total volume of national expenditure allocated to the investment projects necessary for urban renewal, including the infrastructure projects benefiting from the Community aid. The granting of the Community aid is subject to a finding that it is indeed additional to such national expenditure.

Financial provisions

The amount of Community aid may not exceed 70% of the cost of the investment. This limit applies where different Community aids are combined (notably Regional Fund aid).

At the request of the United Kingdom, advances not exceeding 80% of the amount of the Community aid granted for each project may be paid. The balance for each project is after its completion, on receipt of a statement from the United Kingdom Government certifying that the project in question has been completed and that all the payments relating to it have been made.

Procedures

Aid applications are submitted to the Commission in the form of a list accompanied by all the information necessary for the assessment of each project, such as its nature, characteristics and location, the authority responsible, the total cost, the financing arrangements, the schedule of work and expenditure and any other relevant details.

The annual list of projects and the draft Commission decisions concerning the granting of Community aid are forwarded to an *ad hoc* Committee composed of representatives of the Member States.

Decisions are taken by the Commission in accordancce with the procedure laid down for the granting of aid from the European Regional Development Fund.

B. Exceptional financial support in favour of Greece in the social field (Council Regulation No 815/84)

Aim

The aim of this exceptional measure is to contribute to the achievement of Community objectives in the social field and the improvement of the conditions for Greece's access to aid from the European Social Fund.

Main features

The measure, which applies for a period of five years (1984-88), takes the form of Community financial support for:

(a) the construction, adaptation and equipment of vocational training centres in zones not eligible for Regional Fund X aid;

(b) the construction, adaption and equipment of centres for the rehabilitation of the mentally ill and mentally handicapped with a view to their vocational rehabilitation.

The Community financial support is granted to project described in advance in programmes drawn up by Greece. The total amount of support is 120 million ECU over five years.

Eligibility and selection criteria

In the case of centres mentioned above financial support may be granted only for expenditure intended to cover:

(a) the construction of new centres and the extension and adaptation of existing buildings, including the necessary architects' and engineers' fees;

(b) the equipment of centres;

(c) pilot projects to demonstrate the most efficient methods for implementing the programme;

(d) on-the-job training for the adaption of the professional qualifications of medical, therapeutic and para-medical staff and social workers.

Community financial support covers a limited number of centres that are particularly worthy of encouragement.

Financial provisions

Community financial support is granted at a rate of 55% of eligible public expenditure.

An advance equivalent to 60% of the financial support granted is paid on confirmation by Greece that the executiion of the project has begun.

The Commission pays the balance of the financial support on application by Greece within the 12 months following completion of the project.

Procedures

The Greek authorities submit their aid applications to the Comission.

Such applications include all the information necessary for assessing the extent to which the projects for which support is requested conform to the regulation and to the objectives of the Community policy of which they form a part as well as the extimated expenditure and schedules of work and of the corresponding payments.

The Commission decides on the granting of aid after consulting a committee composed of representatives of the Member States.

List of addresses of national government departments dealing with the EAGGF Guidance Section

Belgique/België

Ministère de l'agriculture
Ministerie van Landbouw
Manhattan Center
Office Tower
Avenue du Boulevard, 21
B-1000 Bruxelles

Danmark

Landbrugsministeriet
Slotholmsgade 10
DK-1216 København

BR Deutschland

Bundesministerium für Ernährung, Landwirtschaft und Forsten
Bonner Straße 85
D-5300 Bonn-Duisdorf

ΕΛΛΑΣ/ELLAS

Ὑπουργεῖο Γεωργίας
Ypourgeio Georgias
Ἀχαρνῶν 2
Aharnon 2
ΑΘΗΝΑΙ 102
Athina 102

France

Ministère de l'agriculture
78, rue de Varenne
F-75700 Paris

Ireland

Department of Agriculture
Dublin 2, Ireland

Italia

Ministero dell'agricoltura e delle foreste
Via XX Settembre 20
I-Roma

Luxembourg

Ministère de l'agriculture, de la viticulture et des eaux et forêts 1, rue de la Congrégation
L-1352 Luxembourg

Nederland

Ministerie van landbouw en visserij
Bezuidenhoutseweg 73
NL-2500 EK s'Gravenhage

United Kingdom

Ministry of Agriculture, Fisheries and Food
Great Westminister House
Horseferry Road
London SW1 P2A
United Kingdom

List of addresses of national government departments dealing with the European Social Fund

Belgique/België

Ministère de l'emploi et du travail
Ministerie van Tewerkstelling en Arbeid
Administration de l'emploi
Administratie van de Werkgelegenheid
Rue Belliard, 53
Belliardstraat 53
B-1040 Bruxelles
B-1040 Brussel

Danmark

Arbejdsministeriet
Laksegade 19
DK-1063 København K.

BR Deutschland

Bundesministerium für Arbeit und Sozialordnung
Rochusstraße 1
D-5300 Bonn-Duisdorf

ΕΛΛΑΣ/ELLAS

'Υπουργείο 'Εργασίας
Ypourgeio Ergasias
'Υπηρεσία Σχέσεων μέ τίς Εὐρωπαϊκές Κοι-νότητες (ΥΣΕΚ)
Ypiresia Sheseon me tis Evropaïkes Koinotites (YSEK)
Πειραιῶς 40
Peireos 40
ΑΘΗΝΑΙ – Athina

France

Ministère du travail
Mission du Fonds social européen
14, avenue Duquesne
F-75007 Paris

Ireland

Department of Labour
Mespil Road
Dublin 4, Ireland

Italia

Ministero del Lavoro
Dir. gen. OAPL
Via Flavia, 6
I-Roma

Luxembourg

Ministère du travail et de la sécurité sociale
57, boulevard de la Pétrusse
L-Luxembourg

Nederland

Ministerie van Sociale Zaken
Volmerlaan 1
NL-Rijswijk (Z.-H.)

United Kingdom

Department of Employment
Caxton House
Tothill Street
London SW1 H9NF
United Kingdom

List of addresses of national government departments dealing with the European Regional Development Fund

Belgique/België

Ministère des affaires économiques, expansion économique
Ministerie van economische zaken, economische expansie
Rue de l'Industrie, 10
Nijverheidsstraat 10
B-1040 Bruxelles
B-1040 Brussel

Danmark

Direktoratet for Egnsudvikling
Søndergade 25
DK-8600 Silkeborg

Handelsministeriet
2, afdeling 6, kontor
Slotsholmsgade 12
DK-1216 København K.

BR Deutschland

Bundesministerium für Wirtschaft
Villemonbler Straße 76
D-5300 Bonn-Duisdorf

ΕΛΛΑΣ/ELLAS

Υπουργείο Εθνικής Οικοναμίας
Ministry of National Economy
Πλατεία Συντάγματος
Platia Syntagmatos
ΑΘΗΝΑΙ
ATHINA

France

Délégation à l'aménagement du territoire et à l'action régionale 1, avenue Charles Floquet
F-75007 Paris

Préfecture du département ou de la région.

Ireland

Department of Finance
Government Buildings
Upper Merrion Street
Dublin 2, Ireland

Italia

Ministero per gli interventi straordinari nel Mezzogiorno
Via Boncompagni 30
I-Roma

Luxembourg

Ministère de l'Économie nationale
19, rue Beaumont; B. P. 97
L-Luxembourg

Nederland

Ministerie van Economische Zaken
Laan van N. O. Indië 127
NL-Den Haag

United Kingdom

Department of Industry
Kingsgate House
66 Victoria Street
London SW1 E 6SJ

Department of Environment
2 Marsham Street
London SW1
United Kingdom